LEFT HANDED : RIGHT HANDED

By the same author
Memory Matters

LEFT HANDED: RIGHT HANDED

Mark Brown

DAVID & CHARLES
Newton Abbot   London   North Pomfret (Vt)

British Library Cataloguing in Publication Data

Brown, Mark
   left handed, right handed.
   1. Left-and right-handedness
   I. Title
   152.3'35   QP385
   ISBN 0–7153–7510–5

© Mark Brown 1979

All rights reserved. No part of this
publication may be reproduced, stored in a
retrieval system, or transmitted, in any
form or by any means, electronic,
mechanical, photocopying, recording or
otherwise, without the prior permission of
David & Charles (Publishers) Limited.

Typeset by Northern Phototypesetting Company, Bolton
and printed in Great Britain
by Redwood Burn Ltd., Trowbridge & Esher
for David & Charles (Publishers) Limited
Brunel House, Newton Abbot, Devon

Published in the United States of America
by David & Charles Inc.
North Pomfret Vermont 05053 USA

Contents

Acknowledgements   7

Introduction   9

1 Two Hands   11
Symmetrical or asymmetrical? – Left and right – The mirror problem – Are you right-handed, left-handed or neither? – Handedness: environment or heredity? – Promotion of the right and persecution of the left – Why left-handed? – Advantages and disadvantages of being left-handed – Left and right associations – The bias against the left – Conclusion

2 Two Brains   47
The structure of the brain – Split-brain patients – The right and left hemispheres – The left brain – The right brain – Brains at work – Left-handers – Tests for language – Brainedness and handedness – Male and female – The football machine mystery – Why different brains?

3 Two Worlds   93
The symbolism of left and right – Artist versus scientist – Thought and language – Education – Learning – Specialisation – Getting through – Problem solving – Four-stage problem-solving approach – Creativity – Religion and mysticism – Are opposites opposite? – The individual and society

Bibliography   133

Index   137

Acknowledgements

The author wishes to thank Karen Jennings, Heinz Norden, Jeannine Herron, Tony Buzan, Alyson Corner, Allen Dyer, Nicholas Scott and Peter Russell, who have all helped with the ideas in this book. A special acknowledgement is made to Robert Ornstein, whose book *The Psychology of Consciousness* was of major inspiration, and also to M. C. Corballis and I. L. Beale the authors of *The Psychology of Left and Right*.

Introduction

Why are most people right-handed? Why are only about ten per cent of people left-handed?

You are probably left-brained for language. This means that the left brain primarily processes language. The left brain is usually the centre of mathematical ability, analysis and logic. Why has the left brain developed a preference for these skills in most people? Why is this sometimes reversed in left-handed people? The right brain is more involved with more imaginative thinking and awareness of space, the body and music. Why is the human brain separated into two halves? Are there two brains?

Man, it is argued, is often dualistic in his thinking. He thinks in terms of opposites — light and dark, up and down, past and future, scientific and humanistic, logical and intuitive, reason and emotion, life and death. Why do we think in terms of opposites? Do opposites conflict or complement? Could these extremes represent different types of thinking, each one typical of one of the two brains?

Is there any connection between our being right-handed, strongly left-brained and language and analysis orientated in our thinking? Is our vision of the world a simple reflection of the structure of the brain?

1　Two Hands

Symmetrical or asymmetrical? — Left and right — The mirror problem— Are you right-handed, left-handed or neither?— Handedness: environment or heredity? Promotion of the right and persecution of the left — Why left-handed? — Advantages and disadvantages of being left-handed— Left and right associations— The bias against the left— Conclusion

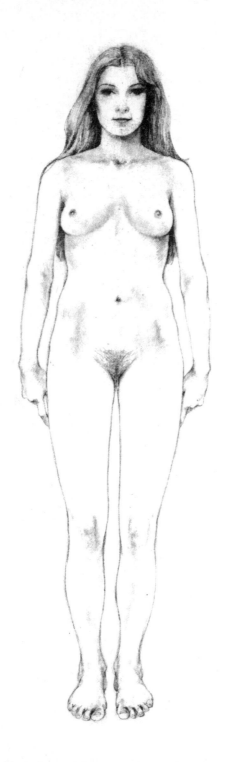

Fig. 1

Symmetrical or asymmetrical?

Look at a naked human being (Fig. 1). One side of the body is practically a duplication of the other. There are two eyes, two nostrils, two shoulders, two arms, two hands, two breasts, two hips, two legs, two feet, and each limb is practically a mirror image of the other.

If we take an illustration of a face and then reproduce two left sides or two right sides so that they can be matched together (Fig. 2) what do we notice?

A face made up of two left sides or two right sides is not quite like the original face. Although there is a superficial symmetry or likeness between the two halves, they are in fact different.

Looking more closely at the body we see that there are often consistent differences between one side and the other. The right arm is often slightly longer than the left and the bones of the left leg are often longer than those of the right. Inside the body there is a shift to the left for the heart, the stomach and the pancreas. With a male, the left testicle is usually lower than the right. The jumble of intestines is decidedly asymmetrical. The right lung tends to be the larger of the two and the liver and the appendix are usually shifted to the right.

In action there is an even more obvious difference between the two sides of the body. We shake hands with the right hand, we make pledges of allegiance and oaths of office with the right hand. We salute with the right arm and hand. Religious gestures are normally right-handed, as when making the sign of the cross. Most people write with their right hand. Many people are also right-footed — for example, they will tend to kick a football with the right foot.

Many people have a dominant eye, usually the right. To test

yourself for 'eyedness', simply look into the distance and fix your eyes on a particular object. Then align the tip of your forefinger with the object at which you are looking. You will notice that there will be two images of the finger-tip. Most people will tend to use the image of the dominant eye. To discover which eye you have chosen close one eye and then the other. The dominant eye, when open, will be directly aligned with the object. The dominant eye will be used in such tasks as aligning gun sights and looking through telescopes and microscopes.

The body is therefore far from perfectly symmetrical. In Part 2 the two halves of the human brain, although almost symmetrical in appearance, will be seen to have different mental abilities.

How symmetrical is the world in which asymmetrical man lives? Examples of asymmetrical creatures include the hermit crab, which has one very large and one small pincer, and the anablebs, a fish which has its sex organs on the side of its body. Honeysuckle climbs in a left-handed way, so as to produce a left-handed helix. (In 1965 the discovery of a left-handed whelk received much press attention. Usually whelks and many other types of shellfish have counterclockwise or right-handed shells.)

Nature does not easily allow us to determine what is left or right. Although it has been suggested that the heart, which is slightly shifted to the left, provides a basic guide, there are, unfortunately, those who have the heart shifted to the right. Similarly if we shine a light through dextrose glucose, the light bends to the right (hence dextrose), but another type of glucose (laveose) bends the light to the left.

Martin Gardner points out in *The Ambidextrous Universe*, that nature does have its own intrinsic handedness. Prior to 1957 scientists considered the labels north and south poles

* J. D. Isaacs, J. W. Stork, D. B. Goldstein and G. L. Wick in *Nature* 253, 1975

Fig. 2(a) A normal asymmetrical face.

Fig. 2(b) Same face but with the right side duplicated on the left.

Fig. 2(c) The same face again but this time with two left sides.

(and therefore left and right) to be purely conventional, and could easily be interchanged with no real effect: '. . . the poles do not really exist. They are just names for the opposite sides of a spin' (Gardner). Experiments conducted by Madam Chien-Shiung Wu showed that when a nucleus of cobalt was cooled a greater number of electrons issued from the south side. And so at this most fundamental level of physics nature is not necessarily symmetrical and can in effect show a handedness.

On a lighter note, even bath water can show a preference for left or right. Undisturbed water running through a plughole north of the equator tends to run out anticlockwise, and south of the equator to run out clockwise. This is because of what is known as the 'coriolis effect', caused by the rotation of the earth.

An even more surprising phenomenon is the way that one of our major left/right conventions affects the atmosphere. Certain research suggests that in the northern hemisphere traffic should drive on the left, and in the southern hemisphere on the right.

> Opposing streams of traffic driving on the right would create an anticlockwise vorticity in the atmosphere which might combine with the natural cyclonic vorticity of the northern hemisphere, increasing the number of tornadoes. There is evidence that the frequency of tornadoes in the United States is indeed influenced by traffic flow – another instance of the polluting influence of the motor car . . .*

Left and right

What is meant by the words 'left' and 'right'? The Oxford Dictionary defines 'left' as 'The distinctive epithet of the hand which is normally the weaker and of the other parts on the same side of the body . . .', and 'right' as 'The distinctive epithet of the hand normally the stronger; by extension also of that

---

* M. C. Corballis and I. L. Beale *The Psychology of Left and Right*

side of the body, its limbs, their clothing . . .' After these basic definitions the reader becomes aware of a definite preference for the right hand – the Oxford Dictionary definition of 'left-handed' continues '. . . awkward, clumsy; ambiguous, double-edged, of doubtful sincerity or validity . . . ill-omened, sinister . . .'.

In English we use the word 'right' to mean correct. Martin Gardner suggests that the word 'left' may have had its origin in the fact that the left hand is little used and therefore very often 'left out' of most tasks. This is probably just one of many reasons why the left hand was in the past (and to some extent still is) the unfavoured hand. We have the expression 'a left-handed compliment'. The word 'sinister' is derived from the Latin word for 'left', while on the other hand 'dextrous', which suggests skillfulness, comes from the Latin word for 'right'.

> The French word for 'left' is *gauche*, which also means 'crooked' or 'awkward'; the French word for 'right' is *droit*, which also means 'just', 'honest' and 'straight'. Our word 'adroit' is based on the French word. In German the word for 'left' is *link* and the word *linkisch* means 'awkward'. The German *recht* for 'right' means 'just' and 'true', as it does in English. The Italian left hand is called the *stanca* which means the 'fatigued', or the *manca*, which means the 'defective'. Spaniards speak of the left hand as *zurdo*, and the Spanish phrase *a zurdas* means 'the wrong way'.*

Thus 'left' and 'right' are not simply neutral words but have developed definite emotive associations.

The French scholar Robert Hertz begins his celebrated essay entitled 'The Pre-eminence of the Right Hand: A Study in Religious Polarity' thus:

> What resemblance more perfect than that between our two hands! And yet what a striking inequality there is!

---

* M. Gardner *The Ambidextrous Universe*

To the right hand go honors, flattering designations, prerogatives: it acts, orders, and *takes*. The left hand, on the contrary, is despised and reduced to the role of a humble auxiliary: by itself it can do nothing; it helps, it supports, it *holds*.

The right hand is the symbol and model of all aristocracies, the left hand of all plebeians . . .

What are the titles of nobility of the right hand? And whence comes the servitude of the left?

The political connotation of left and right is supposed to be based on the original seating arrangement in the French National Assembly. The nobles sat on the King's right hand and the capitalists sat on his left. This suggests a fundamental attraction towards the right. The reasons for the preference for the right are discussed shortly. Today the terms 'left' and 'right' in the United Kingdom are far more 'party' than ideologically based. The Germans have a more ideological conception of left and right.

The idea of left and right is important to human beings only in certain tasks. If a fly lands on my shoulder I do not need to know that the fly has landed on my *left* shoulder. I can have a perfectly good body awareness and control, with no sense of left and right. However, to read, to write, to give and take directions, I need a sense of left and right.

I remember as a child having no instinctive feeling for left and right. I learnt which was my *right* hand because I used to *write* with it – this was the mnemonic I used. And so by means of elimination it became quite easy to establish which was my left hand! Children, when asked which is their left or right hand, may be seen to go through the motions of writing, or in Roman Catholic countries making the sign of the cross, so as to establish the right and therefore the left hand.

The next problem I had was to work out left and right for other people. This always struck me as an unduly difficult task. I adopted the strategy of imagining myself standing behind the person whose left and right I was trying to establish. Piaget (renowned for his work on child psychology) relates the child's ability to tell where left and right are for another person with the growth away from total egocentricity and an increased awareness of other people.

I was glad to discover that I was not alone in my difficulty in establishing left and right. Corballis and Beale relate the case of 'army recruits in Czarist Russia who were so bad at telling left from right that, to teach them the difference, they were drilled with a bundle of straw tied to the right leg and a bundle of hay to the left'. These authors go on to point out that Sigmund Freud, Hermann von Helmholtz, and the poet Schiller also had difficulty in telling the difference. To quote from a letter Freud wrote: 'I do not know whether it is obvious to other people which is their own or others' right and left. In my case in my early years I had to think which was my right; no organic feeling told me. To make sure which was my right hand I used quickly to make a few writing movements.'*

An almost equally famous character also had difficulty: 'Pooh looked at his two paws. He knew that one of them was right, and he knew that when you had decided which of them was right, then the other one was left, but he never could remember how to begin. "Well," he said slowly . . .'**

The differences between the two sides of the body, the slight physical differences or functional differences, are therefore very important in enabling us to tell left from right.

The mirror problem

As I shave in the morning the person who grins back at me from the mirror seems to be reversed left to right but not up and down.

---

* S. Freud *The Origins of Psychoanalysis: Letters to Wilhelm Fliess, drafts and notes: 1887–1902, 1954*
** A. A. Milne *The House at Pooh Corner*

Two Hands

If you stand in front of a mirror and point at the mirror with your right hand, and imagine that the image you see is a real person, that person points at you with his left hand. I have been asking myself for years why, as the hand is turned about from left to right, is it not also turned upside down? When I ask friends this question most grin knowingly, say 'Um' and 'Ah' for a few seconds, then frown and finally reply that it is too long since they studied physics and they can no longer remember the reason which is really very simple. Occasionally I meet somebody who seems to know the answer who may then proceed to blind both of us with jargon.

I tried the following explanation from Martin Gardner's *The Ambidextrous Universe*: [A mirror reverses] 'the structure of a figure, point for point, along the axis perpendicular to the mirror. Such a reversal automatically changes an asymmetric figure to its enantimorph (*mirror image*). Because we ourselves are bilaterally symmetrical, we find it convenient to call this a left-right reversal.' I found I was not much the wiser, and I despaired when reading another account: 'If you look into a mirror, what you see is not really a left-right reflection of yourself, but a *back-front* reflection.'* And so as I shave I reassuringly quote to myself 'Of the "person" who peers back at you out of the mirror, one could say that he or she is a back-front reflection of yourself; it is as though your nose, mouth, eyes and so on have all been pushed through the back of the head, and the back of the head pushed through to the front. One could also say the person is an up-down reflection of yourself, rotated back about a horizontal axis to the upright position.'

Having struggled patiently and finally despaired of these explanations, let me offer my own version.

What does a mirror do? Imagine a ten foot high, four foot wide transparent wall in front of you. This wall is made of

* M. C. Corballis and I. L. Beale *The Psychology of Left and Right*

sticky cellophane. The cellophane is colour-sensitive and will take on the colour of any object pressed against its surface. Stick out your right arm and slowly walk into the cellophane wall. The cellophane stretches and moulds round your body perfectly. At the point illustrated in the diagram, slowly start to walk back out of the cellophane wall. As you walk back you bring the cellophane surface with you. Finally what you will produce is an inverted mould of yourself. This inverted mould is what you normally see in a mirror.

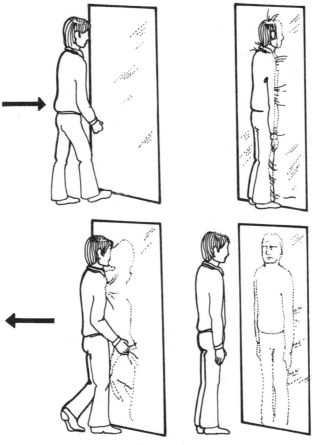

Fig. 3

Two Hands

Does a mirror in fact reverse from left to right?

If you stand in front of a mirror the image you see seems to have your left hand as its right and vice versa. Therefore it might seem that there is a reversal. However, try lying down on the floor facing a mirror (Fig. 4). What do you see? Are you getting a left-right reversal – are your feet where your head is and is your head where your feet are? Hopefully not! So what has happened?

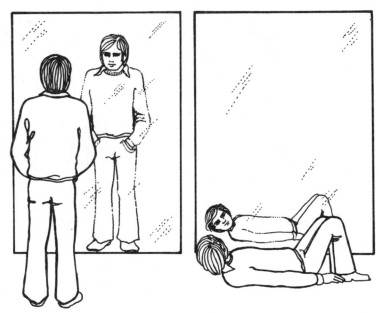

Fig. 4

Try standing in front of a mirror and put your left hand up to feel your heart – which for most people is best felt slightly to the left of the centre of the chest. Your left hand is feeling your heart on your left side. Look at what the person in the mirror is doing – he is holding his heart with what seems to be his right hand on the right-hand side of his body! The very simple question is, which one is real? In fact it is *you* holding your ᴎeart on your left-hand side with your left hand that is real. What you see in the mirror is the inverted mould of yourself. This inverted mould is an image; it is *not a true representation*.

Another way to illustrate this point is to stand in front of a mirror and take your right hand and bite lightly on one of your fingers. The sensation of the teeth is felt by the right finger. The image, however, presents someone who is biting a finger on its left hand. Which one is real? Surely the one getting a bitten finger!

In both these cases confusion arises because the person looking at the image in the mirror presumes that the image has its own left and right. You are in a sense creating a new person **by** doing this. There is no person in the mirror. There is simply an image. If you believe that image to be reversed, it is only reversed because you are giving it its own sense of left and right.

Imagine a mirror with seeing eyes. The mirror sees you as others see you. However, the image you see in the mirror is not what other people see.

For a moment return to the cellophane wall idea. There are two ways to explain how you could use the cellophane wall to see yourself as others see you. The first goes as follows and is the simpler of the two. Put out your right arm again and slowly walk into the cellophane film (Fig. 5). Stop when your body is almost completely immersed. At this point you and the cellophane are frozen. This freezing process takes away the stickiness of the cellophane. You are pulled out of the mould. The cellophane shape that we now have, when viewed from the other side, is how other people see you.

The second way to illustrate how the cellophane wall can show you what you look like to the rest of the world is as follows. As before, walk into the cellophane wall. As on the very first occasion, after your body has been fully enveloped, slowly begin to walk out from the cellophane. This time the cellophane is sticky and therefore comes out with you (Fig. 6).

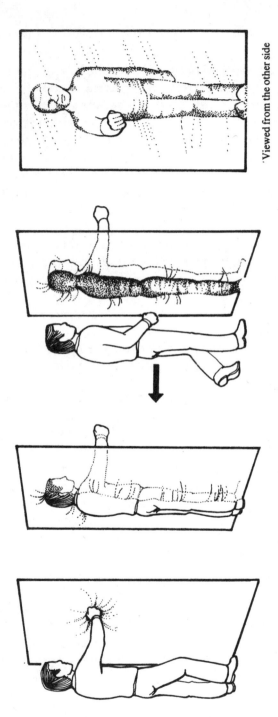

Fig. 5

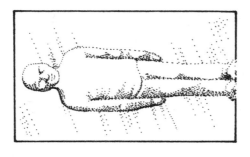

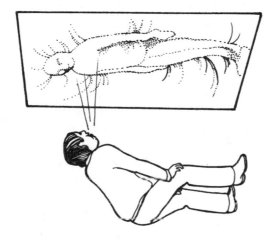

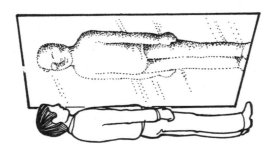

Fig. 6

Viewed from the other side

Because the cellophane is colour-sensitive it takes on all the colouring of your body. The mould that you have made gives you the image you see in the mirror. What you need to do is to blow very hard at the cellophane so as to turn the mould inside out. You have now, on the other side of the cellophane, reproduced an image of what people actually see when they stand in front of you.

It can be an interesting experience to stand by the side of someone you know very well, both of you looking in a mirror. Looking closely you notice slight differences in the mirror image of the person as compared with their real selves. Because we are what is called bilaterally symmetrical the differences are very slight. If you have a beauty spot on your left cheek it will appear on the right in the mirror – but generally the image you get in a mirror is not very different from what you get in a photograph.

The possible difference between the real and the image has been highlighted since the acquisition of our cat. Most of his face is white. His head and ears are black and the black fur comes down in an inverted 'V' shape over his eyes. I turned round to catch a mirror image of the cat as he admired himself in the mirror. So different was the mirror image, that I thought a stray had moved in. The mirror image gives a very different impression.

The problems about left and right being reversed only occur when you start thinking of the person in the mirror as being a representative of yourself. It is a representation, but only to a limited extent – what you in fact see is (the image form of) the cellophane mould as in the first diagram. Because there are usually only a few differences between the left-hand and right-hand sides of the body, we find it easier to refer to this whole phenomenon as left-right reversal.

The creator of *Alice in Wonderland*, Lewis Carroll, 'was handsome and asymmetric – two facts that may have contributed to his interest in mirror reflections. One shoulder was higher than the other, his smile was slightly askew, and the level of his blue eyes was not quite the same.'*

Would it matter if we lived in a *Through the Looking-Glass* world, where everything was reversed left to right? If we were brought up from birth in a reverse world it would not matter. The greatest difficulty if we, like Alice, moved into a mirror world would be that of reading and writing. Our eyes for many languages have to read from left to right (left and right confusion is associated with reading difficulties). Apparently Lewis Carroll was a part-time mirror writer. Leonardo da Vinci is perhaps the most renowned mirror writer. He was left-handed.

Martin Gardner suggests that mirror writing is often easier for left-handed people. Many right-handers also find it easier to mirror write with their left hands if they write simultaneously as they would normally with their right. For certain people mirror writing is easier than normal writing. This may be the case even though the writer subsequently has difficulty reading back what he or she has written without the aid of a mirror. Corballis and Beale point out that mirror writing 'often accompanies a switch from one hand to the other'.

Martin Gardner refers to an interesting experiment where fifty scenic photographs were 'flopped'. This simply means that the image was reversed so as to produce a *Through the Looking-Glass* effect. A slight preference was shown by the subjects of this experiment for the non-flopped, the normal, as opposed to the reverse view. It would be interesting to give the same test to Tweedledee and Tweedledum and the other characters of *Through the Looking-Glass*. When next in natural surroundings you might try to see what difference you would notice if everything around you were reversed left and right.

* M. Gardner (ed) *The Annotated Alice* (original text, Lewis Carroll) (Penguin revised edition, 1970)

Two Hands

If a mirror does not in fact reverse your face from left to right
– at least that is what I have maintained – why if you write your
name on a piece of paper, in block capitals, and then hold it up
to the mirror, is it reversed left to right?

Are you right-handed, left-handed, or neither?

Various researchers have stated that between one and thirty
per cent of the world is left-handed. Other estimates suggest
that between five and twelve per cent of the population either
are, or consider themselves to be, left-handed.

The difficulty that has dogged research results is the lack of
consistency in definitions of left- or right-handedness. Criteria
have included the mother's opinion of the child's handedness,
the writing hand, the more skilled hand in specialised tasks, the
throwing hand, the steadier of the hands, the hand with the
faster reaction time, and so on. One system of analysis involves
the following tests to establish which hand is the lead hand:
writing, drawing, striking a match, sweeping with a broom,
taking a lid off a box, using a knife, using a spoon, using
scissors, brushing teeth and throwing. * I had always presumed
that I was right-handed, and yet trying all ten of these tests, I
found that the right-hand bias was not as strong as I had
presumed.

Some people seem to be very strongly left- or right-handed.
Some are surprisingly ambidextrous. Certain individuals prefer
to use the left hand for certain tasks and the right for others.
However, in the past, and to an extent today, people tend to
have thought of themselves and others as being either left- or
right-handed. Much past research can no longer provide very
useful data as handedness was often established on this simple
basis of left or right and often judged simply by the subject's
own opinion: today '. . . most investigators view handedness

* Oldfield's *Edinburgh Handedness Inventory 1971*

as a graded characteristic that is best conceptualised as varying along a continuum from individual to individual, as opposed to being considered as a dichotomous or trichotomous variable' (ie left- or right-handed or ambidextrous).*

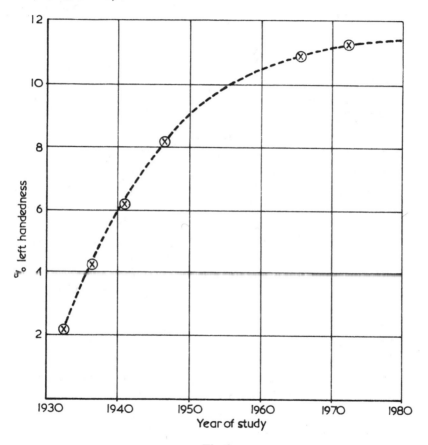

Fig. 7

* Alan Searleman, 'A Review of Right Hemisphere Linguistic Capabilities', *Psychological Bulletin* 1977, Vol 84 No 3, 503–28

There is evidence from one US study to suggest that the number of left-handers is on the increase. The following graph (Fig. 7) shows the increase in the number of left-handers (on the basis of writing hand) from 1932 to 1972.*

Jerry Levy comments that 'suggestions that stuttering and other emotional problems might result from forcing a child to switch handedness have produced a lessening of this pressure over time, so that at present most American children are allowed to use whichever hand they choose for writing'. Some researchers have suggested that George VI might have developed a stammer because his rather strict governess at Buckingham Palace insisted that he changed his writing hand.

There is evidence to suggest that slightly more females are right-handed than males. One survey found two to three per cent more left-handers among boys than girls.

In the Old Testament, Judges 20, verse 16, there is the reference to the 700 left-handed men in the army of Benjamin, who made up part of the total army of 26,000. This gives a percentage of 2.69. This low percentage of 2.69 may be partly explained by a bias that has certainly in the past existed against the left which we will look at shortly. Furthermore there is 'the consideration that there is no evidence that the other 26,000 soldiers were all right-handed'.**

Today, with only between five and fifteen per cent of the world being self-confessed left-handers, there is obviously a major tendency towards right-handedness. Why has the right hand become dominant for many people? Do other animals show a dominant hand, limb or paw preference? The answer is that they do – once an animal has established a preference for one paw or the other it will tend to stick to it – but there is no general right or left preference. If you take 100 rats or mice,

* Jerry Levy, 'Psychobiological Implications of Bilateral Asymmetry' in *Hemisphere Function in the Human Brain* by Stuart J. Dimond and J. Graham Beaumont

** Curtis Hardyck and Lewis F. Petrinovich, 'Left-Handedness', *Psychological Bulletin* Vol 84 No 3, May 1977

fifty will tend to be left-pawed. And so the original choice seems to be fairly arbitrary. Once the choice has been made it tends to be adhered to. Research on animals suggests that pawedness can be predicted, for example, by the architecture of the cages in which the animals live. Placing food so that it is more easily reached with the left paw usually results in left-paw dominance.

There seem, however, to be two exceptions to the general rule that most animals show no overall preference for handedness. Cats show a slight left-paw preference and African mountain gorillas have shown a slight right-handed preference.*

As other animals show no strong preference for one side or the other, why is it that human beings show a general preference for the right? This strong right-handed tendency has been found in tools made by primitive man. In cave drawings the face is often drawn turned to the left, which some consider to be an indication of right-handedness. One piece of research is based on a study of forty-seven fossil baboon skulls. It seems that the baboons had been killed as food by Australopithecus. The researchers found that seven of the skulls had been fractured on the left side by blows from the front, 'indicating that the implement used to strike the blow had been held in the assailant's right hand. Only two skulls were found with similar fractures on the right side.'**

Handedness: Environment or Non-environment?

Environment. Some researchers argue that environmental factors have encouraged or even determined this right-hand dominance. Many societies have worshipped the sun, and to follow the path of the sun in the northern hemisphere the body moves from left to right. And so a very early association could have been made between the sun – the life giver – and the right side of the body and the right hand.

* M. C. Corbalis and I. L. Beale *The Psychology of Left and Right*
* *Psychological Bulletin* Vol 84 No 3, May 1977

... the earth, to those facing the magnetic north, itself revolves from left to right, and therefore the sun rises in the east. The sun, being light itself, was the earliest object of worship, from pagan times to the first chapter of the Gospel according to St John, which attributed the gift of light to God Himself ... From these simple, primal facts has emerged such a wealth of ritual and superstition that it would need an entire book to enumerate them all. From the earliest times, to go *with* the sun's course was not only lucky, but compulsory, to combat the evil spirits.*

One major objection to this theory is that the right hand is and has been dominant in the Australian hemisphere. However, J. Chelhod in his essay in the book *Left and Right* points out that '... a glance at the map of the world shows that the major part of the habitable surface of our planet, the different centers of the great classical civilizations and perhaps also the cradle of humanity, is found in the northern hemisphere. It is from here that great waves of migration would have set out ... Therefore it seems quite normal that well-established notions should accompany man in his gradual trek ...'

Several physical and emotional factors have been used to explain the tendency towards right-handedness. There is what is now known as the 'sword and shield' theory

... the choice of the right hand as the preferred one might have been dictated by the fact that the heart is displaced slightly to the left so that the left hand was assigned the passive, protective role of holding the shield while the right hand wielded the stick or sword.**

Other physical arguments include the suggestion that the right-hand side of the body is more powerful than the left (Aristotle) and Sir Francis Bacon suggested that the liver being

---

* Michael Barsley *The Left-Handed Book*
** M. C. Corballis and I. L. Beale *The Psychology of Left and Right*

predominantly positioned on the right side of the body is the basis for handedness.*

An even more ingenious argument was suggested by Professor Buchanan in the nineteenth century. He suggested that because there was a slightly greater weight on the right-hand side of the body (because of the liver and lungs) it is easier for a person to balance on his left foot. The right hand would be left free for action and so with time the right hand and arm muscles would develop more than those on the left.**

One argument stresses that many skills only need one hand. It is therefore not surprising that one hand has developed slight dominance over the other. While the left hand holds, the right hand operates. An environmental argument was presented by Plato who suggests that handedness was a question of bad habit: 'In the use of the hand we are, as it were, maimed by the folly of our nurses and mothers, for although our several limbs are by nature balanced, we create a difference in them by bad habit.' (Book VII Plato's *Laws*.)

Non-environment. Many researchers suggest that handedness, at least right-handedness, is genetically based. Signs of handedness have been observed from birth on. Children who later become right-handed have been observed to have a definite pattern of handedness in the first year of life. Such a pattern is difficult to explain as an environmental product.

Among those destined to become right-handed, the earliest observable preference, at about 16 to 20 weeks of age, was usually for the *left* hand. This was followed by a period of ambilaterality, then a preference for the right hand at about 28 weeks. A repetition of the cycle produced a general preference for the left hand at about 36 weeks, then a preference for the right hand at 40 to 44 weeks. Cyclic

* *Psychological Bulletin* Vol 84 No 3, May 1977
** Michael Barsley *The Left-Handed Book*

changes tended to recur, although dominated increasingly by a preference for the right hand, up until about eight years of age, by which time all the subjects were consistently right-handed.*

Handedness can also be predicted in part by what is known as the 'tonic neck reflex'. This reflex has the following characteristics: '. . . the head is turned to the right or the left, the arm and the leg on the side to which the head is turned are extended, and the opposite arm and leg are flexed. Most children show a right tonic reflex, which means they turn their heads to the right.'** The direction of the reflex has proved to be a reasonably good indicator of subsequent hand preference.

An interesting survey into the possibility of a genetic basis for handedness was carried out among people with the name Kerr (Karr). The Kerrs, especially in Scotland, have had a reputation for left-handedness. Apparently 'Ker-handit' and 'carry-handed' are descriptions of left-handed people. Castles built by the Kerr family have a high instance of anticlockwise spiral staircases. (This anticlockwise spiral aids a left-handed swordsman defending his castle.)

The author of the following anonymous verse evidently felt that the Kerrs' reputation for left-handedness was of some antiquity:

But the Kerrs were aye the deadliest foes
That e'er to Englishmen were known,
For they were all bred left-handed men,
And fence against them there was none.

To try to establish if there is a higher-than-average incidence of left-handedness in the Kerr family, the *Journal of the Royal College of General Practitioners* invited doctors to send in

* M. C. Corballis and I. L. Beale *The Psychology of Left and Right*
** M. C. Corballis and I. L. Beale *The Psychology of Left and Right*

34

information concerning the handedness of any Kerrs who were their patients. As happened with left-handed whelks, the press gave much coverage to this survey both in Britain and North America. As a result, not only did doctors supply information but also individual members of the Kerr family sent in details of handedness. The results of the study are shown below and, as the *Journal* pointed out, 'there is a significantly greater number of left-handed or ambidextrous people in the sample whose surname is Kerr than in the control sample'.

	Kerr/Carr family	Control family	Total
Right-handed	141	178	319
Left-handed & ambidextrous	59	22	81
	200	200	400

One further interesting observation is that male Kerrs, who are now living abroad showed a greater tendency to be left-handed or ambidextrous. As the *Journal* pointed out, 'Whether left-handedness and a tendency to emigrate are genetically associated remains to be speculated upon!'*

Other explanations for handedness include anatomical differences between the two halves of the brain (discussed later) and vascular supply to these two halves. Other theories consider foetal position, birth order and brain damage. The human brain is divided into two halves or two hemispheres. There is a certain relationship between the speech orientated side of the brain (for most people the left) and the dominant, right hand. The genetic influence on handedness and 'brainedness' is discussed in the section on the two halves of the brain (see p. 81).

* *Journal of the Royal College of General Practitioners* 1974, 24, 437–9

Two Hands

Promotion of the right and persecution of the left

Some writers argue that the left hand, being slightly weaker (due to genetic/anatomical/environmental/emotional factors or whatever), has become an object of persecution. This persecution, especially in the past, has encouraged most people to become right-handed. The greatest exponent of this theory is Robert Hertz:

> For centuries the systematic paralysation of the left arm has, like other mutilations, expressed the will animating man to make the sacred predominant over the profane, to sacrifice the desires and the interest of the individual to the demands felt by the collective consciousness, and to spiritualize the body itself by marking upon it the opposition of values and the violent contrasts of the world of morality ... Dualism, which is essential to the thought of primitives, dominates their social organization ... All the oppositions presented by nature exhibit this fundamental dualism. Light and dark, day and night, north and south ... How could man's body, the microcosm, escape the law of polarity which governs everything?*

Hertz is therefore arguing that man originally was prone to think in opposites and the pairing of these opposites with left- and right-handedness was a natural development. As Clarke puts it: 'the human body is always treated as an image of society and there can be no natural way of considering the body that does not involve at the same time a social dimension.'**

Why Left-handed?

One reason given in the past for left-handedness was 'emotional negativism'. A general distrust of left-handedness

---

* Robert Hertz, 'The Pre-eminence of the Right Hand' in *Right and Left* (ed R. Needham)
** Mary Douglas *Natural Symbols*

probably reached a peak in the ideas of Cesare Lombroso, an Italian psychiatrist and criminologist. It was his theory that there were to be found more left-handers than usual in prisons. He argued that left-handedness tended to be a sign of the born criminal. As Martin Gardner points out, these views are today discredited. However, Gardner goes on to make an interesting point about the possible conflict that could have developed between a strongly left-handed child and its parents at a time when left-handedness was at best frowned upon. 'It is easy to understand how such conflict might have led to difficulties that would predispose a person towards crime.' Another report on handedness* suggests that there is a slight continuing bias against left-handedness. To quote *The Times* of 10 August 1976:

> ... recent study comparing left and right-handed 11-year-olds from a large national sample of the population showed considerable and significant differences between teachers' reports on left-handers and the results of objective tests. Teachers reported a greater tendency amongst left-handed pupils towards poor control of their hands, 'bad writing' and speech which was 'difficult to understand'. Subsequent tests showed the differences to be unfounded.

The article goes on to point out that these misconceptions are to an extent understandable, for example because a left-hander appears to write in an 'odd' position.

Brain damage has been offered as an explanation for a minute instance of left-handedness. Some research shows that there may be slightly more left-handers than right-handers who suffer from undetected brain damage. This percentage is undoubtedly very small. The explanation for this relationship may be that there is a cross over in the human body, the left side of the body being predominantly controlled by the right

* Developmental Correlates of Handedness in a National Sample of 11 Year Olds', *Annals of Human Biology* 1976, Vol 3 No 4, 329–42

side of the brain and vice versa. If for some reason, early in life, the left brain is damaged the right brain will tend to take over certain functions of the left brain, of which (right) handedness is usually one.

Another explanation for left-handedness is that the individual has not inherited the usual right-handed bias. In fact, he may have inherited no bias at all which can give rise to a very ambidextrous individual. Left-handedness is sometimes an indication of a different brain organisation, which will be considered in the section on handedness and 'brainedness'. Finally environmental factors cannot be ignored. Much of the child's learning is based upon imitation of those around him. If his parents are left-handed the child may naturally start to carry out tasks in a left-handed fashion.

Advantages and Disadvantages of being Left-handed

Barsley's book *A Left-Handed Man in a Right-Handed World* sets out some of the disadvantages of being left-handed in a world that is primarily geared for right-handed people. For example, there are problems with scissors, irons and potato peelers. Today there are left-handed scissors, left-handed irons, left-handed potato peelers and even left-handed moustache cups. There is a shop for left-handers in London.

Although the left-hander may not find life as convenient as the right-hander, many left-handers are noted to be more ambidextrous than right-handers. This is hardly surprising considering the social stress on right-handedness. Such ambidextrous ability is obviously an advantage in sport and in manipulative tasks like surgery and playing a musical instrument.

Many famous tennis, baseball and cricket players are left-handed. Martin Gardner argues that to be left-handed is an advantage for a baseball player and for professional black jack dealers! Generally a left-hander may be at an advantage in many sports because his opponent is not used to the unfamiliar response of his opponent. Particularly in baseball, 'the layout of the baseball diamond gives left-handed batters an advantage: they are nearer first base when they stand at the plate and have a shorter distance to run after a hit.'* Leonardo da Vinci, Michaelangelo and Hans Holbein are examples of artists who were left-handed.

For reasons that will become clear after the consideration of brain organisations of left- and right-handers there can be definite advantages for a left-hander in terms of recovery from brain damage (hopefully not a common occurrence), and in the words of a recent research project on left-handedness: ' "two heads are better than one" might well be applied to the unique advantage possessed by many of the left-handed.'**

Left and right associations

If your left ear is itching or going red, someone is said to be maligning you. If it is your right ear, someone is said to be speaking well of you. Similarly, if your left hand is itching, money, according to another superstition, is about to part from you, and if the right is itching, money will come to you.

What reasons are there for the preference for the right? There is the already mentioned idea of sun worship. Robert Graves in *Greek Myths* relates a myth (probably of Greek origin) in which Uranus is castrated. The son who castrated him grasped his genitals with his left hand and so did little to further the left hand's reputation. Later the Romans adopted the Greek belief that the left hand was the hand of ill omen. The Romans 'began employing slaves whose sole duty was to make sure guests entered the master's home right foot first — the origin, say some, of our word footman'.†

* R. H. Bailey *The Role of the Brain*
** *Psychological Bulletin* Vol 84 No 3, May 1977
† Beverly Hayne in *Psychology Today* September 1976

The Bible shows a definite preference for the right hand. Perhaps the most marked example of this comes in the Vision of Judgement in Matthew 25:

> ... and before him shall be gathered all nations: and he shall separate them one from another, as a shepherd divideth his sheep from his goats:— And he shall set the sheep on his right hand, but the goats on the left. Then shall the King say unto them on his right hand, Come, ye blessed of my Father, inherit the kingdom prepared for you from the foundation of the world ... Then shall he say also unto them on the left hand, Depart from me, ye cursed, into everlasting fire, prepared for the devil and his angels ... And these shall go away into everlasting punishment: but the righteous into life eternal.

Psalms also abound with references to the right hand, and at Christ's crucifixion the good robber was on his right. Barsley suggests that the Bible contains over a hundred positive references to the right hand but very few to the left.

Corballis and Beale point out that 'In the Pythagorean tradition among the ancient Greeks, for example, the right is associated with the odd numbers, the one, the male, the light, the straight, the good, while the left is linked to the even numbers, the many, the female, the dark, the crooked, the evil.'

Left-handedness has been seen as a trait of witches. Supposedly one of the earliest signs that a baby is destined to become a saint is the way he will reject the left breast! Rings are worn on the left hand so as to protect this more vulnerable side. We throw salt over our left shoulder so as to keep the devil away. People who are clumsy we call cack-handed, which means left-handed. (In fact there are several expressions for left-handed — clicky-handed in Cornwall, coochy in Dorset, squippy in Wiltshire, cuddy-wifte in Lancashire, and kay-neived and dolly-pawed in Yorkshire.)

Certain African tribes, in an account written in 1906, adopted the following procedure: 'If a child should seem to be naturally left-handed the people pour boiling water into a hole in the earth, and then place the child's left hand in the hole, ramming the earth down around it; by this means the left hand becomes so scalded that the child is bound to use the right hand.'* A further example is given in 'Nuer Spear Symbolism', an essay by Evans-Pritchard in which he mentions that the Nuer youths would put the left arm out of action for months or even years by pressing metal rings into the flesh of the left arm from the wrist upwards. The rings were pressed in so tightly that sores and great pain resulted, thus rendering the arm useless.**

Heinz Wieschoff in his essay 'Right and Left in African Cultures'† stresses the general associations between the right and the good, the left and the bad. For example, the left hand is not used for eating. One very good reason (at least historically) may have been hygiene. It is argued that right-handed people would normally use the left hand for genital and anal cleansing; and use the right hand for eating. For one tribe in Sierra Leone

> The rule is that the right hand serves the upper half, particularly the mouth, and the left hand serves the lower half, particularly the genitals and anus. Food must be conveyed to the mouth only by the right hand, and when washing the region of the mouth after a meal again only the right hand may be used. As far as possible, in the preparation of food women must avoid handling it with the left hand. When cleaning the anus only the left hand may be used. Also, in the case of men engaged in sex play only the left hand may touch the woman's genitals.††

> Twitching of your right eyelid indicates that some absent member of your family will come back or that some other pleasant event is in store for you, but a twitch of your left eye

---

* H. A. Wieschoff in *Right and Left* (ed Needham)
** *Right and Left*
† *Right and Left*
†† James Littlejohn in *Right and Left*

means that a member of your family will die or that you will have some other sorrow . . . if a person when travelling hits his right foot against something it is a good omen and that good news and good food may be expected at the journey's end; the same occurrence in regard to the left foot, however, would be regarded as a warning not to continue the trip.*

In another essay from *Right and Left* Alb Kruyt refers to the belief that if the left eye of a corpse stays open a close member of the family will die, whereas if the right eye remains open a distant relative of the deceased will be affected. Littlejohn mentions that 'While on the road a bush rat jumping across one's path . . . announces success (from left to right) or failure (right to left)'.

One means of investigating whether the prejudice against the left continues is to use what is called the semantic differential test. People are asked to rate a word – in this example the word 'left' – on a scale of word opposites:

Left

Good		X	Bad
Female	X		Male
Strong		X	Weak

The person being tested is asked to make a mark at the point which best shows his or her associations with the word at the top of the chart. The test was carried out on a group of American undergraduates:

Details and statistics aside we can make a long story short by saying the students' ratings were overwhelmingly in agreement with the anthropological and psycholinguistic literature . . . The Left was characterized as bad, dark, profane, female, unclean, night, west, curved, limp,

* E. Westermarck *Ritual and Belief in Morocco*

homosexual, weak, mysterious, low, ugly, black, incorrect, and death, while the Right meant just the opposite – good, light, sacred, male, clean, day, east, straight, erect, heterosexual, strong, commonplace, high, beautiful, white, correct, and life.*

When children were given this test, their bias against the left was found to increase as they grew older.

There is some evidence that the assocations with left and right may be shown in the profiles artists paint in their portraits. In one particular survey over a thousand portraits painted over the last 600 years were examined. Sixty per cent were found to be painted in the left profile, sixty-eight per cent of the women were shown to display more of the left cheek than of the right, compared with only fifty-six per cent of the men.**

The bias against the left

As mentioned above, one good reason for the taboo against the left is the question of hygiene. Because the left hand was the unclean hand it was more susceptible to association with the profane and impure. Hertz argues that primitive man naturally thought in terms of opposites, for example male and female. 'How could man's body, the microcosm, escape the law of polarity which governs everything? Society and the whole universe have a side which is sacred, noble, precious, and another which is profane and common; a male side, strong and active, and another, female, weak and passive; or, in two words, a right side and a left side . . .'

One reason for the basic distrust of the left may be a general bias against minorities. Another reason is possibly based on the slightly increased incidence of language disability in the case of left-handers. This very small group is probably largely made up of would be right-handers who are suffering from

* William Domhoff in *The Nature of Human Consciousness* (ed Ornstein)
** M. C. Corballis and I. L. Beale *The Psychology of Left and Right*

slight brain damage and have switched to the left hand. Therefore, right handers who have shifted may have been helping to give the left hand a bad name.

Conclusion

An interesting summary of the development of handedness comes in the essay by William Domhoff quoted above:

> If we now return to our earlier comments on handedness, we can see how possible it is that dichotomous thinking may have fastened on to the slight genetic tendency for right bilaterality and increased that tendency by investing it with a good-bad, active-passive, and potent-castrated polarities that pervade so much of our thinking. Reinforced by the functional need for specialisation due to tool use, and embedded in language and mythology, these infantile psychodynamics helped to select for hereditary right handedness and to convert the ambidextrous and uncommitted. It became a right handed world, with the percentage of left handers increasing only during wars, depressions, and Left (permissive) epochs.

The author goes on to explain this last curious point by suggesting that these periods were times of greater tolerance and therefore perhaps demanded less conformity.

Over the last twenty years research has shown that the two halves of the human brain have relatively different functions. The left is more involved with language and reason, whereas the right is more involved in acts of imagination and more creative types of thinking. In the body there is a physical cross over in the nervous system. The left brain controls the right half of the body, and vice versa. In most people and certainly in nearly all right-handers it is the left brain that controls language. It is also the left brain that controls the right hand. Why did this specialisation develop, and does it help us to understand the dominance of the right hand?

The research on the two halves of the brain has also been interpreted to suggest that every individual potentially has artistic and scientific types of mental skills. Some people seem to develop much more of one side than the other. These are some of the considerations discussed in Part 2.

Hertz and others have suggested that the human mind naturally tends to think in opposites — light and dark, good and bad, male and female, etc. Do these opposites simply reflect the simple opposites that we use in language, or do they reflect a more fundamental difference in man's perception — perhaps reflecting the different types of thought and experience of the two halves of the brain? This and general philosophical ideas will be the subject of Part 3.

2   Two Brains

The structure of the brain — Split-brain patients — The right and left hemispheres — The left brain — The right brain — Brains at work — Left-handers — Tests for language — Brainedness and handedness — Male and female — The football machine mystery — Why different brains?

"Let me introduce you to my right-hand man . . . and my left-hand man."

The structure of the brain

What is it about the human brain which seems to make man more successful than the other animals? The size of the brain was once considered to be very important. Obviously if an animal had a very small brain and a very large body, most of the brain might be occupied by controlling the physical movements of the body. *Stegosaurus*, which was a dinosaur with a brain about the size of a cat's brain and a body thirty feet long, became extinct while other animals survived. Possibly the relative smallness of his brain contributed to his lack of success.

Is man's success simply due to his brain size? Whereas the human brain weighs around 1450g, the brains of elephants and whales are several times heavier than this. One factor may be that a larger body needs a larger brain to control it. In fact humans, with a brain-body ratio of about 1:50, have larger brains in proportion to their body size than whales. The simple brain-body ratio seems to be an inadequate guide to mental ability; mice have a similar brain-body ratio to humans, while that of sparrows is actually higher. One reason for this is that

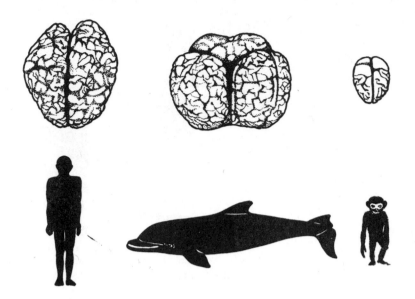

Fig. 8 The comparative brain sizes of man, dolphin and chimpanzee.

'smaller animals need relatively more brain than larger ones "as basic equipment" '. Taking this into account a scale called the Pallium Index has been produced, on which man comes out at 170, big whales at 150, the Indian elephant at 104 and mice at 2.* It is exciting to consider that other animals may have as high an intelligence potential as man. Research with dolphins has shown that they communicate using a relatively sophisticated 'language', and the American neurologist John Lilley believes that man and dolphins may one day be able to communicate with each other.

The human brain is divided into two halves which are almost physically symmetrical (Fig. 6). The cerebral cortex forms the upper surface of the brain. The two halves (sometimes called hemispheres) of the cerebral cortex are joined together by the corpus callosum, made up of some 200 million nerve fibres.

* Erwin Lausch *Manipulation*

50

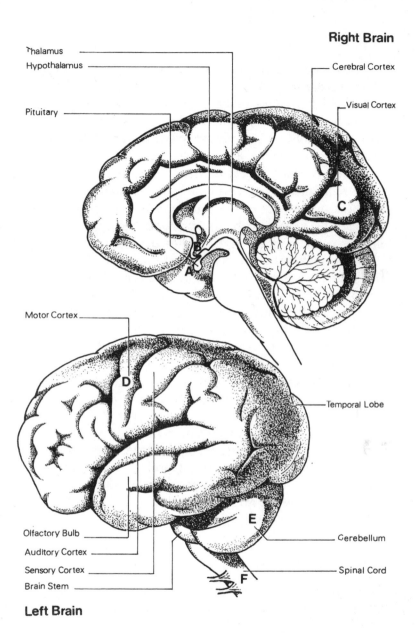

Right Brain

Thalamus

Hypothalamus

Pituitary

Cerebral Cortex

Visual Cortex

C

A

B

Motor Cortex

D

Temporal Lobe

Olfactory Bulb

Auditory Cortex

Sensory Cortex

Brain Stem

E

F

Cerebellum

Spinal Cord

Left Brain

Fig. 9

The cortex contains some seventy-five per cent of the 10–12 billion neurons in the brain. The cortex is associated with 'the capacity for language, the delicate motor control that makes possible the use of tools, the safety devices that manage built-in drives and emotions, interpretive systems that enable man to perceive himself and the world around him'.* The cortex is the area where thinking processes take place.

The right side of the cortex is largely responsible for the control of the left side of the body, and vice versa. So when a pianist plays a note with his left hand, the original motor impulses come from the right side of the cortex.

The fact that the human brain is made up of two halves (as in other animals) was noted by Hippocrates in about 400BC. For a long time it was presumed that the functions of the brain were equally distributed – for example, both sides would be responsible for language, etc. Largely from observation of patients with brain damage, as early as 1745 it was noted that a stroke affecting the left brain resulted in almost total loss of language. Although the capacity for language had been virtually lost, the patient in question was still able to sing certain hymns which had been learnt prior to the stroke, suggesting that speech was centred in the left hemisphere and more musical abilities were centred in the right brain. In 1864, Hughlings Jackson, an English neurologist, reported of a woman with a tumour affecting the right hemisphere that 'she did not know objects, persons and places'. It was almost 100 years before these observations were really tested.

Split-brain patients

The corpus callosum is the bundle of nerve fibres connecting the two hemispheres. To try to limit the wild spread of nerve signals associated with acute epileptic seizures, certain neuro-

* R. H. Bailey *The Role of the Brain*

surgeons cut the corpus callosum. This operation in many cases was successful. What was very surprising was the lack of apparent change in personality and mental ability. It was even joked that the sole purpose of the corpus callosum was to keep the hemispheres from caving in!

Roger Sperry, a leading figure in 'split-brain' research began testing split-brain patients in the early 1960s. Shortly after the corpus callosum had been cut, the behaviour of a typical patient was described as follows: '... on awaking from the surgery the patient quipped that he had a "splitting headache", and in his still drowsy state he was able to repeat the tongue twister "Peter Piper picked a peck of pickled peppers".' However, definite changes were noted. It was observed that the left-hand side of the body very rarely showed any spontaneous activity: 'when he brushed against something with his left side he did not notice that he had done so, and when an object was placed in his left hand he generally denied its presence.'*

The observation of over a century before, that speech seemed to be controlled by the left brain, started to be confirmed – when an object was placed in the right hand of a split-brain patient in such a way that he could not see it, the patient was able to describe and name the object. Because of the crossover in the nervous system, the right hand is controlled by the left brain. When an object was put in the patient's *left* hand without him being able to see it, he was usually unable to describe it. This did not mean that the patient was unaware of what the object actually was – the difficulty was in actually describing the object in language. The object could be identified, however, in a non-verbal test. For example, the patient could match the object in his hand with the same object in a varied collection of other objects. 'Though the right hemisphere could register what the left hand was holding, it could not make its owner speak about it. To do so, it would

---

* Michael S. Gazzaniga 'The Split Brain in Man' *Scientific American* Aug 1967

have needed co-operation with the speech-skilled left hemisphere, with which there was now no connection.'*

Visual tests on split-brain patients provided even more data. To explain the experiments fully, it is necessary to consider how the signals from the eyes are fed to the two hemispheres or brains. The left sides of the light- and colour-sensitive parts of the eyes, the retinas, connect to the left brain, while the right sides of the retinas are connected with the right hemisphere. Because of the way the rays of light from the left cross over to the right-hand side of the retina as they pass through the pupil of the eye, the view to the left of the centre of the field of vision is fed initially to the right hemisphere and the view to the right of centre is initially fed to the left hemisphere. However, in the normal brain the information on one side is almost immediately available to the other side through the communication channel of the corpus callosum. In split-brain patients, however, there can be no such direct communication.

With a split-brain patient a picture which appeared left of centre would go only to the right brain, and a picture to the right of centre would register only in the left brain. In one experiment the word *heart* was flashed up on a screen in front of a split-brain patient so that *he* was left of centre and was therefore picked up by the right side of the retina and so fed to the right brain. *Art* was to the right of centre and so was picked up on the left sides of the retinas and so fed to the left brain or hemisphere (Fig. 7).

If you and I were involved in this experiment, we would immediately have recognised the word *heart*. However, a split-brain patient, when asked which word he had just seen, would reply *art*. *Art* would have been picked up by the left brain, which could give a verbal reply for what it had seen. However, if the patient were asked to identify the word he had seen by pointing with his left hand to one of two cards on which were

* Erwin Lausch *Manipulation*

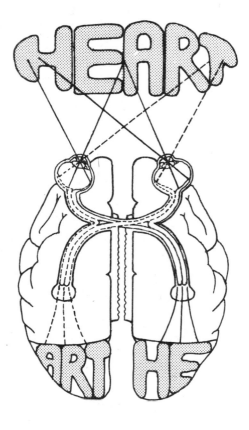

Fig. 10

written *he* and *art*, the left hand would point to *he*. The left hemisphere could give a verbal response to what it had seen, while the right hemisphere could only give a physical response for what it has seen.

After the operation, split-brain patients found that although they retained their ability to write with their right hand they had lost much of their ability to draw. For example, if a patient were asked to copy a square with his right hand he might be able to draw the corners but was almost incapable of joining the corners together so as to complete the square. The left hand, however, could draw and could copy a square (Fig. 11).

55

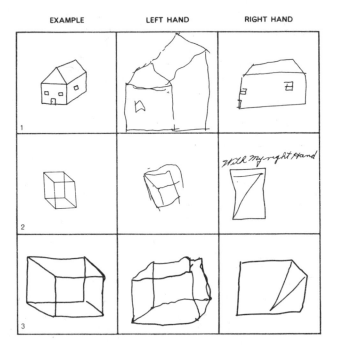

EXAMPLE	LEFT HAND	RIGHT HAND

Fig. 11

The left brain very quickly showed itself to be dominant for language. This does not mean, however, that the right brain is illiterate. The ability of the right hemisphere to comprehend language is illustrated in a series of experiments where split-brain patients were asked to retrieve objects concealed in a bag with their left hand. In one case the patient was asked to pick from the bag 'the fruit monkeys like best'. The left hand could quite easily pick out a banana from the selection of assorted fruit in the bag. The researchers 'knew that touch information from the left hand was going exclusively to the right hemisphere because moments later, when the patients were asked to name various pieces of fruit placed in the left hand, they were unable to score above a chance level'.*

The two brains, as well as having specialised abilities, were

---

* Michael S. Gazzaniga 'The Split Brain in Man' *Scientific American* Aug 1967

also shown to have wills and emotions of their own. One example of this was when a picture of a naked woman was flashed to a young housewife's left hemisphere. She immediately identified the picture. When the same picture was shown only to her right hemisphere, she blushed, squirmed and finally started chuckling. When pressed to describe what she had seen, she replied: 'I do not know . . . nothing . . . oh – that funny machine.' Although the right brain could not respond verbally, it certainly did emotionally.

In the ordinary human brain, information in one hemisphere becomes available to the other via the corpus callosum. Normally the two brains appear to work in a very integrated manner. Even in split-brain patients, Sperry discovered, the two brains could learn to communicate in a very subtle way. One experiment involved the flashing of a green or red light in the patient's left visual field – which would therefore go to the right side of the retina and to the right hemisphere. The patients were asked to guess which colour they had seen. Because the information had gone to the right hemisphere and only the left hemisphere could speak effectively, it was expected that the score would be no better than that of a person guessing with his eyes closed. However, when the patient was allowed a second guess he began to score above the level of chance. When he had guessed incorrectly the patient would frown or shake his head and then choose correctly. The right hemisphere (which knew the colour) was apparently able to pass information by frowning and nodding over to the left hemisphere which was then able to guess correctly.

One researcher concludes that 'our studies seem to demonstrate conclusively that in a split brain situation we are dealing with two brains, each separately capable of mental functions of a high order'.* Having established that there are effectively two brains, researchers started to see whether or not

---

* Michael S. Gazzaniga 'The Split Brain in Man' *Scientific American* Aug 1967

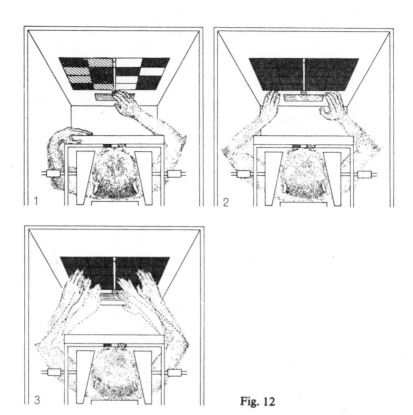

Fig. 12

the split-brain patient had twice the normal ability to handle information. Research on monkeys suggests that this is the case. The diagram below shows that split-brain monkeys can handle more visual information than normal monkeys (Fig. 9). There is one major difference between the operation carried out on humans and monkeys – in the case of monkeys, the visual channels are cut in such a way that the information from one eye is fed exclusively to one hemisphere.

Split-brain humans in certain experiments were able to carry out tasks twice as quickly as normal humans. However, the tests were such that this ability would be of little use in everyday life. Furthermore, the lack of communication between the two brains can cause definite problems. One

58

patient for a time after the operation found that he had developed 'quarrelsome hands' – while he was trying to pull up his pants with one hand the other one would be trying to take them down! This same potential conflict was illustrated where a patient was asked to arrange coloured blocks according to a given diagram. Because he could see the bricks fully, both brains were receiving information. The patient was asked to use only one hand at a time. His left hand, controlled by the right brain, which tends to be the more gifted of the two when it comes to awareness of space, could arrange the blocks quickly. The right hand (controlled by the left hemisphere, which although well developed for speech has comparatively weak spatial awareness) had great difficulty with the task. The right brain could see what was going on, and accordingly the left hand kept coming to the rescue. Finally, to stop this interference the patient had to sit on his left hand!

'All the evidence indicates that separation of the hemispheres creates two independent spheres of consciousness within a single cranium, that is to say, within a single organism. This conclusion is disturbing to some people who view consciousness as an indivisible property of the human brain.'*

The right and left hemispheres

These experiments supported Hughlings Jackson's suggestion that the speech centre for most people is to be found in the left brain. To be exact, 'it is estimated that 90–99 per cent of all right-handers have their language functions predominantly sub-served by the left hemisphere. Similarly, it is estimated that 50–70 per cent of non-right-handers also have their language functions localised primarily within the left hemisphere.'**

---

* Michael S. Gazzaniga 'The Split Brain in Man' *Scientific American* Aug 1967
** Alan Searleman 'A Review of Right Hemisphere Linguistic Capabilities' *Psychological Bulletin 1977, Vol 84 No 3*, 503–28

Left-handers who do not fit into this pattern will be discussed shortly.

Although the two halves of the brain are practically physically symmetrical, different functions or specialisations are found in each one. Split-brain research and other clinical evidence portrays the left brain as logical, verbal, with mathematical and general scientific abilities. What therefore was the function of the right hemisphere? As late as 1961 one researcher was still considering the possibility that the right brain might be merely a 'vestige' – although this particular commentator said that he would rather keep than lose his right brain!*

The left brain is often referred to as the dominant hemisphere, and the right as the minor hemisphere. The right hemisphere, however, seems to be superior in spatial awareness, non-verbal communication, awareness of the body's orientation in space, and musical ability. Why should the right hemisphere or brain therefore have been considered the minor of the two? One explanation for this must lie in the importance which we attach to speech. Both hemispheres have highly specialised abilities, and it can be argued that both are equally important. One reason why the left brain was considered dominant is because it is the verbal hemisphere – it can talk! The right brain has difficulty expressing itself verbally, and therefore cannot articulate its abilities. The left hemisphere seems to have more control over the bodily function on both the left and the right sides than does the right hemisphere. Many researchers argue that it is more appropriate, however, to regard both hemispheres as dominant as they both have essential roles.

Many insights into bodily and mental functioning have been based on the study of illness and injury. The initial findings

* J. Z. Young 'Why do we have two brains?' in *Interhemispheric Relations and Cerebral Dominance* by V. B. Mount Castle

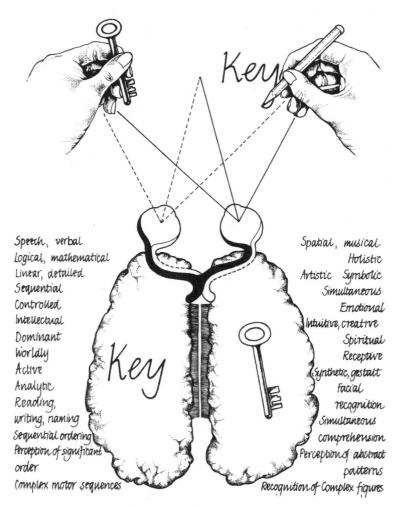

Speech, verbal
Logical, mathematical
Linear, detailed
Sequential
Controlled
Intellectual
Dominant
Worldly
Active
Analytic
Reading,
writing, naming
Sequential ordering
Perception of significant
order
Complex motor sequences

Spatial, musical
Holistic
Artistic Symbolic
Simultaneous
Emotional
Intuitive, creative
Spiritual
Receptive
Synthetic, gestalt
Facial
recognition
Simultaneous
comprehension
Perception of abstract
patterns
Recognition of Complex figures

Fig. 13 The specialised abilities of the two hemispheres of the human brain.

about the functioning of the two brains were largely based upon split-brain patients. This division of the two brains is a very radical operation. Therefore it might be unwise to assume the same mental make-up for the intact human brain. To validate the initial findings on split-brain patients researchers therefore began testing other individuals. An outline of the various types of research follows.

Unilateral electric shocks Unilateral electric shock involves temporarily 'knocking out' one hemisphere. It is therefore possible to observe a patient operating with only one hemisphere. By placing the electrodes on the right of the patient's head, researchers have therefore observed a person working with only the left hemisphere. To summarise one research report, the person with only the left hemisphere functioning retains his power of speech and is even described as more talkative than usual. However, it has been noticed that intonation tends to be less expressive and the voice is described as having a 'nasal twang'. Furthermore, the left brain tends to have a reduced awareness of other people's intonations and has difficulty in distinguishing between male and female voices. The subject loses much of his musical ability. He retains theoretical knowledge learnt earlier in his life – predictably, as this type of knowledge is largely obtained through language. His awareness of time and space changes, and he may not recognise rooms that he knows well:

> Sometimes the 'left hemisphere' person even looks out of the window at the leafless trees and the snow drifts and is unable to say immediately whether it is winter outside or summer. Indeed, if he answers that 'January is a winter month' this is merely a formal inference and not a result of direct visual impression. Thus, although the verbal orientation of the 'left hemisphere' person is unimpaired, his visual orientation in space and time is seriously disturbed.*

In contrast, the person operating with his right brain only is noticeably less talkative. Vocabulary seems to be reduced. Comprehension of speech is reduced. Sentences, if used, tend to be short. Responses are more often made in gestures. He can distinguish perfectly well between male and female voices. He recognises songs and can hum them perfectly well. His

* *The Unesco Courier* Jan 1976

perception of images is perfectly normal. Non-verbal memory remains the same. As with the person whose left brain only was working, the patient whose right brain only is functioning also finds that his perception of time and space is changed. He may recognise the room he is in but fail to realise its purpose. Generally the right hemisphere person 'manifests an impairment in those aspects of mental activity which are the basis of abstract, conceptual thinking, while those aspects linked with imaginal thinking have been retained and even improved'.*

A slightly different technique can be used to knock out one of the two brains. Instead of using the electric shock one of the hemispheres can be drugged, usually by injecting sodium amatyl.

Brain damage Although patients suffering from brain damage cannot be described as 'normal', in the past they have often provided useful insights into the functions of the two brains.

Damage to the right hemisphere can have the effect of reducing 'the ability to remember music, nonsense figures, and faces, and to perform a variety of nonverbal, visual spatial tasks'.** The composer Ravel, having suffered damage to his left brain with resulting loss of speech, retained his musical ability. In adults, damage to the left brain usually results in the loss of speech.

Hearing tests The left and right brains each receive input from both ears. However, the left ear has a better connection with the right brain than with the left brain, and the right ear has a better connection with the left brain than the right brain. The crossed connections are stronger than the uncrossed ones.

A typical listening test might consist of listening to a particular melody in one ear and a different melody in the other

* *The Unesco Courier* Jan 1976
** M. C. Corballis and I. L. Beale *Psychology of Left and Right*

ear. The subject is then asked to select the melody he has just heard from a series of melodies that he listens to afterwards. Melodies which were heard by the left ear were usually more easily picked out than those presented to the right ear. The input from the left ear was predominantly to the right hemisphere.

Visual tests A picture flashed to the left visual field will go to the right of both retinas and therefore to the right hemisphere. If you flash the image just for a split second, only one brain will be directly stimulated. For most people words and letters are described most accurately when they are flashed in such a way that the left brain is stimulated. Using this same type of test, the right brain was far superior in spatial tests.

Brain waves The history of the electroencephalogram (EEG) is an interesting one. A German, Hans Berger, fascinated by extrasensory mental ability and in particular telepathy, hoped to show that electrical impulses in the brain could form the basis for telepathic communication. He therefore set about trying to record this electrical activity. In the mid-1920s, by placing electrodes on the head, he did in fact record such activity. The signal that Berger recorded operated at ten cycles a second, which became known as the alpha rhythm. The cycle changed according to mood, attention and mental task.

This alpha rhythm is particularly predominant where the mind is relaxed. In one sense the alpha wave activity can be seen as the brain idling. These electrical patterns in the brain have been recorded while people are involved in different types of tasks, some involving verbal ability, others involving awareness of space. Where a person is involved in a verbal task the alpha rhythm tends to increase in the right hemisphere. This suggests that the right hemisphere is in part being turned off. This turning off may reduce interference between the two brains. In a task involving spatial awareness the left brain shows increased alpha activity – suggesting that the right brain is at work.

'In general, clinical work has found verbal and arithmetical functions (analytic, linear) depend on the left hemisphere while spatial relations (holistic, gestalt) are the special province of the right hemisphere.'*

The left brain

'The left hemisphere is predominantly involved with analytic thinking, especially language and logic. This hemisphere seems to process information in an ordered sequence, which is necessary for logical thought since logic depends on both sequence and order.'** It would be misleading to presume, however, that the left and right brain are specialised to work with a particular type of material – for example in the case of the left hemisphere with words. Certain psychologists argue that each brain is geared to the particular type of thinking or cognitive style – 'the left for an analytical, logical mode for which words are an excellent tool'.† The left brain seems to process information in a serial way – that is to say, one bit of information after another. Understanding speech involves an analysis of one word after another, and emission of speech involves putting one word after another – both serial processes.

Recent research has suggested a far more fundamental division between the left and right brain than simply verbal and non-verbal specialisation. Research on babies, particularly at the University of British Columbia, suggests that the specialisation of the brain is innate and does not depend upon the learning of language. The left brain, in the case of babies tested, was particularly prone to analysing information which

* R. H. Ornstein *Physiological Studies of Consciousness*
** R. H. Ornstein in *Psychology Today* May 1975
† David Galin 'Implications for Psychiatry of Left and Right Cerebral Specialisation' *Archives of General Psychiatry* Vol 31, Oct 1974

involved the recognition of some relationship between a stimulus and a past experience. 'As examples of this type of referential processing the left hemisphere would be more involved than the right in the processing of speech by a human [listener], in the processing of melodies by an experienced musician and printed words by a literate person.'* Earlier on it was suggested that the right brain was particularly involved in the processing of music, but musically experienced listeners often recognise simple melodies better when the information is primarily fed to the left brain. At first sight this would seem to conflict with existing evidence, but an experienced listener is probably involved in a great deal more analysis of the information and therefore it seems appropriate that in fact the left brain is at work as well as the right brain. This research therefore suggests that the left brain deals with information in an analytical and sequential way and also in a comparative and referential manner.

The left brain has been described as being 'unable to see the wood for the trees'. The analytic speech-orientated approach can impede getting a good overall grasp or an overall 'gestalt'. A synthesising whole-grasp approach seems to represent the cognitive style of the right brain.

The right brain

Since the beginning of the 1960s the comparatively mute right brain has aroused increased interest. This one-time 'vestige' 'appears to be primarily responsible for our orientation in space, artistic talents, bodily awareness, and recognition of faces. It processes information more diffusely than the left hemisphere does and integrates material in a simultaneous, rather than a linear, fashion.'** The right brain in most adults

* *The Canadian Journal of Neurological Sciences* 4(3), 203–7
** R. H. Ornstein in *Psychology Today* May 1975

shows itself to be superior at depth, image, pattern and face perception. It is much involved in pitch perception.

Some researchers describe the right brain as the more creative. When given a word it tends to produce an association less common than that produced by the left brain. 'We take the finding of a greater variability and ingenuity in the right hemisphere to indicate the greater participation of the right hemisphere in the creative aspects of thought, attributing to it in this aspect a specialised role. This role is seen as concerned with the more inventive, exploratory and improvisatory aspects of mental activity.'* Images, an often encountered feature in creative thinking, have also been associated with the right brain. It has been argued that when very strong imagery is used in speech, the images will tend to be processed by the right hemisphere.

The right brain has also been associated with dreaming. One reason for this is that dreams are usually highly image ridden and creative as opposed to analytical and verbal. There have also been reports of people who have received damage to the right brain who have said that they have stopped dreaming. Quite often split-brain patients say that they have stopped dreaming, but this is probably due to the lack of communication between the two hemispheres.

One interesting report suggests that people who are involved in more analytical thinking, as for example accountants, lawyers, etc, are less likely to remember the dreams they have than those involved in more imaginative work – for example, artists. A 'convergent' type of thinking seems to epitomise the left hemisphere while more 'divergent' thinking characterises the right.

The relationship between images and the right brain may relate to the difficulty many people have in recalling early childhood memories. If the left brain is seen as the language

---

* S. J. Dimond and G. J. Beaumont *Hemisphere Function in the Human Brain*

system, and the right brain as a more visual system, the right brain will record information from very early infancy. Language coding, however, will start only later on in a child's life. One experiment involved the drugging of the left brain and then showing the right brain particular objects. Later on the subject was unable to remember what objects had been shown although he was able to recognise them again when presented with a mixed set of objects. 'Early childhood memories may be available in the visual system, but inaccessible through the verbal system.'*

Mathematical ability has been primarily associated with the left hemisphere. In some tests on split-brain patients the right brain alone has been able to perform calculations. These findings are obviously confusing to researchers who have associated calculating and mathematical ability with the left brain. However, one suggestion is 'that the capacity of the right hemisphere in dealing with spatial events may be related to the capacity for calculation or numerate abilities.'** In fact it is hardly surprising that mathematical ability involves probably both left and right brain abilities – the left providing the analysis and the right, very often, providing some form of visual recall or blackboard type construction in the mind on which calculations can be worked out.

As in the case of musical awareness, it would seem that both the left and the right brains have their own special abilities to bring to bear on any particular input or problem. Co-operation between the brains is discussed below and seen as absolutely essential.

It appears that for the first six or more years of a child's life both the left and the right brains are involved in language. The taking on of speech by the left brain takes place later on in the

---

* John Seamson 'Coding and Retrieval Processes' in *Hemisphere Function in the Human Brain* by S. J. Dimond and G. J. Beaumont
** S. J. Dimond and G. J. Beaumont *Hemisphere Function in the Human Brain*

child's life. The adult right brain can respond to printed or spoken nouns, but has difficulty with verbs. Its syntax is weak.* A recent review of the capability of the right hemisphere pointed out that while the right is not very good at expressing itself, its comprehension is quite reasonable. It was pointed out that some aspects of speech are, in fact, better handled by the right hemisphere. 'In addition, there is evidence that other linguistic features of speech, such as intonation contours and pitch processing, are not only processed bilaterally but are often handled better by the right hemisphere.'** This research ties in with the earlier observation that a patient operating with left hemisphere only had a 'nasal twang' when talking. The pitch of an individual's voice can also be seen as a musical aspect of speech and therefore involving the right hemisphere.

An interesting insight into the right hemisphere's speech ability comes from one particular patient whose left hemisphere had been removed. The patient was asked to name the number indicated to her. She could, in fact, only do this if she was allowed to count from one up to the number being pointed at. This highlights the way that the right hemisphere is not specialised in dealing with analytical tasks and has to rely upon a whole grasp or gestalt approach.

While the left brain, in a split-brain patient, tends to have the main control of conscious activity, the right brain has been associated with the unconscious. Because of this association at least one researcher has suggested that, because of the physical crossover in the nervous system, the left-hand side of the body might be more prone to psychosomatic disorders. '... Freud, Ferenczi and other early analysts observed that the left side of

---

* Michael S. Gazzaniga 'Cerebral Dominance Viewed as a Decision System' in *Hemisphere Function in the Human Brain* by S. J. Dimond and G. J. Beaumont
** Alan Searleman 'A Review of Right Hemisphere Linguistic Capabilities' *Psychological Bulletin* 1977, Vol 84 No 3, 503–28

the body, controlled by the right hemisphere, reflected more unconscious conflict than the right, including hysterical paralysis.'*

A recent comparison has been made between split-brain patients and many pyschosomatic patients. One researcher suggests that certain people who are psychosomatically unwell create a functional split between the two hemispheres.** Some researchers argue that the build up of unprocessed energy in the right hemisphere can create physical illness.

In conclusion, the right hemisphere's abilities therefore emerge as holistic, non-referential and integrative. Whereas the left brain tends to process information serially, one bit after another, the right brain is geared to the processing of parallel information — dealing with several bits of information at the same time. For example, the recognition of a pattern or a face is fairly instantaneous and does not usually involve the linear or sequential analysis of speech and logic. It is also important, however, to consider the type of input and output of the hemispheres. For example, recent studies suggest that 'If only visual recognition is called for, even if the material is verbal, it is the right hemisphere which acts. If, however, a verbal transformation is demanded, even if the material is non-verbal, it is handled by the left hemisphere.'† And so although the left hemisphere can generally be considered superior for language and the right hemisphere considered superior for synthesising material and being able to see the total rather than the parts, the type of response called for will also affect which hemisphere will process the input.

---

* *Brain Mind Bulletin* Vol 2 No 18, Aug 1977
** *Psychoanalytic Quarterly* 46, 222–4
† 'Hemispheric Specialisation in Commissurotomized Man' *Psychological Bulletin* Vol 81 No 1, Jan 1974

Brains at work

The two brains have been described as 'two semi-independent information-processing units with different specialities'* Many researchers stress that the two brains complement each other. In fact, to a limited extent the right brain possesses left brain specialities, and vice versa. For example, it was seen above that both brains might be involved in the processing of music and in mathematical tasks. 'In many respects the problem of how the two hemispheres work together is a similar one to the nature of activities in a marriage. Each partner has his or her own specialisations, there is a division of labour and divided responsibilities. There may be a dominance of one partner over the other and either conflict and tension or harmonious interaction may result.'**

Certain tasks are best approached logically (left brain), others in a more visual, 'whole grasp' way. In fact the adoption of a logical approach for a visual problem may well result in failure. In Part 3 a visual problem-solving approach will be introduced. Ornstein points out that 'Although it is *possible* to process complex spatial relationships in words, it would seem more efficient to use visual–kinesthetic images. For example, consider what most people do when asked to describe a spiral staircase; they begin using words, but quickly fall back on gesturing with a finger.'†

Possible interference between the two styles of thinking may provide some reason why the hemispheres have specialised for different tasks. The visual synthesising approach might often be in direct conflict with the more verbal analytical approach. Therefore, if both these abilities were to develop fully the brain needed to locate the specialised ability in different parts of the brain and so minimise the clash of incompatible styles of

---

* R. H. Ornstein *The Psychology of Consciousness*
** S. J. Dimond and G. J. Beaumont *Hemisphere Function in the Human Brain*
† R. H. Ornstein *Psyiological Studies of Consciousness*

thinking. Some researchers argue that the brain switches from one hemisphere to the other through a system of inhibition. For example, it has been noticed that split-brain patients usually show greater language ability in their right hemisphere than do 'normal' patients. One argument for this is that in the normal intact brain, the left hemisphere may try to inhibit any attempt by the right hemisphere to deal with language. Obviously this inhibition cannot take place where the corpus callosum has been cut.

So each one of us seems to have 'two computers sitting side by side, each interacting with the world, providing a surface on which information can be received, each proceeding with analysis of the information and checking off its functions against the other, ultimately linking and cross-comparing the products'.*

The brain picture that emerges from this description is that of *two major* hemispheres whose abilities complement each other.

Can the hemispheres come into conflict? Earlier on there was the description of the split-brain patient's hand-conflict in pulling up and taking down his trousers. There was also the block-arranging experiment where the patient had to sit on his hand to stop it interfering. There was also the case of the female split-brain patient who was exposed to a picture of a naked woman. Her right brain reacted in what might be described as an almost unconscious way – she blushed. Some researchers have pointed out that this behaviour is rather like the phenomenon of repression: 'According to Freud's early "topographical" model of the mind, repressed mental contents functioned in a separate realm that was inaccessible to conscious recall or verbal interrogation, functioning according to its own rules, developing and pursuing its own goals . . . and insinuating itself in the stream of ongoing consciously directed

---

* S. J. Dimond and G. J. Beaumont *Hemisphere Function in the Human Brain*

behaviour.'* Some researchers suggest that the right brain may provide location for 'unconscious mental contents'.

How could the two brains come into conflict under normal circumstances? One suggestion goes as follows: imagine a child who is being told by its mother that 'I love you' and yet the mother's behaviour, gestures and expressions suggest that at that moment she feels hatred for the child. The left brain will be picking up the verbal information and the right brain the visual. And so the two brains are in direct conflict. If this type of experience often occurs, the brain may attempt to minimise the crossover of information so as to avoid conflicting signals.

Could poor communication between the two brains account for schizophrenia? Although for a long time researchers have argued against the idea that schizophrenia may be caused by lack of co-ordination between the two halves of the brain, recent findings have indicated that this may be a factor. Testing 'suggests a deficit of integration between the hemispheres, a form of disconnection syndrome'.**

One researcher suggests that there may be a relationship between schizophrenia and right-hemispheric activity. Julian Jaynes, author of *The Origin of Consciousness in the Breakdown of the Bicameral Mind* argues the following points:

Firstly, whereas most of us show in total a slightly more left hemispherical activity than right, the reverse is observed in schizophrenia patients. A schizophrenic shows slightly more activity in the right hemisphere. Whereas the non-schizophrenic tends to switch to and fro between the hemispheres about once a minute, switching in schizophrenics only occurs about once every four minutes. This suggests 'that schizophrenics tend to "get stuck" on one hemisphere or the other and so cannot shift from one mode of information processing to another as fast as the rest of us. Hence their

* *Archives of General Psychiatry* Vol 31 Oct 1974
** S. J. Dimond and G. J. Beaumont *Hemisphere Function in the Human Brain*

confusion and often illogical speech and behaviour in interaction with us, who switch back and forth at a faster rate.'

The same author draws a definite relationship between hypnosis and the right hemisphere. He suggests that there may be a relationship between people who can be easily hypnotised and those people who are particularly reliant upon their right hemisphere. Secondly, he suggests 'several recent studies have found that individuals who manifest these characteristics (ie creative spatial thinking and vivid imagery – ie right hemisphere) more than others are indeed more susceptible to hypnosis'.

The specialisation of the hemispheres is a process that takes place during childhood. If an adult's left brain is damaged he may well lose his power of speech. In a child this may not necessarily be the case at all. The remaining brain in the case of a child may be perfectly capable of taking on the new ability. Much research has suggested that the adult brain loses this flexibility. However, it would be wrong to presume that the situation was hopeless for adults. 'In 1966 neurosurgeons at the University of Nebraska reported on a patient of 47 who, after removal of the left hemisphere, had learnt to speak, sing, write and read again.'*

According to Pavlov, the famous Russian researcher:

Experience clearly shows that there are two categories of people: artists and thinkers, between whom there is a sharp distinction. On the one hand, the artist grasps reality in its entirety as a complete, living and indivisible entity. On the other hand, the thinkers divide up reality, temporarily making it into a kind of skeleton, and only later do they gradually reassemble its parts and thus try to breathe life into it . . .**

* Erwin Lausch *Manipulation*
** *The Unesco Courier* Jan 1976

It is interesting to speculate how far this distinction parallels the distinction between the types of thinking of two brains. 'We should not pretend to understand the world only by intellect; we apprehend just as much by feeling. Therefore the judgement of the intellect is, at best, only half of truth, and must, if it be honest, also come to an understanding of its inadequacy.'*

In Part 3 the ability to use and integrate both types of thinking is seen to be essential in creative thinking.

Left-handers

Whereas nearly all right-handers will process language in the left brain, probably only about sixty per cent of left-handers process it in the left. With most right-handed people damage to the left brain usually results in almost total loss of speech. This is as expected. However, in the case of a left-handed person, whose left brain is damaged, speech may not be affected at all. Even if speech is affected, recovery is often much more successful. The reason for this is that speech in the case of some left-handers may not be located in the left brain — instead it may be in the right. In other left-handers, speech may be found to be more generally distributed throughout both brains. It has also been noticed that a right-handed person who has left-handed relatives may also recover from a left-hemisphere injury faster and more completely than might otherwise be expected. This again suggests that in certain cases there is a more diffuse location for language.

To the chagrin of some left-handers, the research has also pointed out that whereas perhaps only ten per cent of the population is left-handed, fifteen per cent or more of epileptics and mental defectives are left-handed. 'These results suggest that there is an equally reduced incidence of strong consistent

* Carl G. Jung

dextrality [right-handedness] in both the schizophrenic and manic-depressive syndromes.'* The magazine *New Scientist* in 1973 carried an article which reported on a group of forty-seven hospitalised alcoholics. Among this group were three times the normal proportion of left-handers and ambidextrous people usually found in the US population.

Jeannine Herron, a researcher into handedness and brain organisation, points out that this group in part is probably made up of 'damaged right handers who shifted'.** By this she means that this group is in part made up of would-be right-handers whose left brain has suffered some injury, for example, possibly oxygen starvation during birth, and therefore the right brain has taken over hand-control and because of the physical crossover in the nervous system, the left hand will be used. Brain damage, however, will only account for a very low instance of left-handedness.

It seems difficult to ignore the strength of the argument which stresses that handedness is difficult to explain simply in environmental and cultural terms. Although right-handedness may have originally been culturally or environmentally encouraged, the preponderance of right-handedness is difficult to explain solely in terms of the bias against the left and the present day environmental favouring of the right. The almost universal tendency towards right-handedness, as seen in various parts of the world, for example among American Indians and in African tribes, suggests that there is more than simply a cultural or environmental bias towards right-handedness. As Annett (a major figure in handedness research) has pointed out, the origins of right-handedness are therefore likely to be biological rather than cultural.†

The fact that the hemispheres of a right-hander may be more specialised than the two hemispheres of a left-hander may

---

* Pierre Flor-Henry
** *Psychology Today* Sept 1976
† M. C. Corballis and I. L. Beale *The Psychology of Left and Right*

partly explain the possible relationship between some left-handedness and reading and speech difficulties. The relationship which may exist between being left-handed or ambidextrous and reading difficulties does not seem to be an aspect of left-handedness so much as an indication of lack of brain specialisation. However, the different type of brain organisation of some left-handers may have other major advantages. Some researchers have suggested the possibility of greater integration between visual and verbal types of thinking in such people.

The earlier advantage found in some left-handers of easier and fuller recovery from damage to either hemisphere is explained in the way that language may be distributed more equally throughout the two hemispheres. The greater integration of the two styles of thinking in left-handers, although it may have its drawbacks, could give rise to a completely different perception of the world. It would be interesting in future to study those individuals who are found to have speech spread diffusely throughout the brain.

Recent research at the University of California has noticed that left-handers tend to score better on tests involving pitch memory. In particular, the group of moderate left-handers scored best in identifying tones. One argument put forward to explain this is that musical awareness may be spread more equally throughout both hemispheres.*

Although there appears not to be any difference in the intelligence levels of left- and right-handed people, some recent research carried out at the California Institute of Technology suggests that left-handers may on average be better at carrying out certain verbal tasks, but may do less well on tasks involving spatial awareness. It could be that the left-handers have their language skills more diffusely distributed throughout the brain, thus interfering with the spatial functions

* *Science* Vol 199, p559

of the right hemisphere. One researcher noted that in a sample of university students eleven per cent were left-handed, and of these only six per cent were art students, whereas eighteen per cent were law students. However, these findings differ somewhat from those of another survey which suggested a greater than average proportion of left-handers among a sample of architects.

The entire brain organisation of the left-handed or ambidextrous person can be more diffuse than that of the right-handed. Beaumont gives the following analogy:

> The brain of the right-hander is seen as rather like a campus in which books and journals are kept in departmental libraries. These libraries are connected by well organised pathways, but are nevertheless some distance apart. The brain of the non-right-hander is more like a campus which has no large central library in which all books and journals are stored, and which has a cataloging system which makes even relatively related subjects somewhat diverse within the confines of the library building ... In simple terms, the diffuse system, that of the left-hander, carries an advantage for complex integrative operations, but a disadvantage for rapid simple communications ...*

Tests for language

Various ways of establishing which brain is dominant for speech have already been mentioned – electroencephalograph readings, visual tests, listening tests, localised electric shocks, etc. Although less reliable, there are some amusing and simple tests you can carry out on yourself to obtain a rough idea of which brain is speech-dominant.

One very simple test is pencil balancing. Simply try to balance a round pencil on the index finger of one hand at a time. As soon as you have the pencil more or less balanced then

---

* S. J. Dimond and G. J. Beaumont *Hemisphere Function in the Human Brain*

start talking. Marcel Kinsbourne, the originator of this test, suggests that right-handers can balance the pencil for longer with their left hand while they are talking. The reason for this is quite simply that when trying to balance the pencil on the right hand and talk, both actions involve the left brain and, can therefore overtax the brain. It is interesting to note that the balancing time of the left hand increased when the person being tested was talking at the same time. This suggests that the left hemisphere, if not 'kept busy' may tend to interfere. When the left hemisphere was kept busy, by talking, it seems that interference was reduced as balancing of the left hand was improved.

An observation that left-handers can make is as follows: 'There tend to be two types of left handed writers – those who write with the hand in the same type of position as a right-hander and those who write with their hands in hook style.' One researcher suggests that 'those left-handers who adopt the hook style may have language functions represented primarily in the left hemisphere, while those who do not may have language localised mainly in the right.' Those who had the apparently more relaxed writing position tended to have speech more in the right hemisphere. However, this observation awaits further testing.

Another indication of which brain is dominant for speech is provided by hand gestures during conversation. 'Right-handers make many more such gestures with their right hands than their left. Left-handers make more bilateral free movements, which is consistent with other evidence that left-handers show less cerebral lateralization than right-handers do.'*

Another test concerns eye movements. If someone is asked a verbal question – for example, give the meaning of the word 'democracy' – the eyes, some researchers argue, will normally

* M. C. Corballis and I. L. Beale *The Psychology of Left and Right* and D. Kimura 'The Asymmetry of the Human Brain' *Scientific American* March 1973

shift from centre to right; if the question is more visual – for example, describe the face you see on a fifty-pence piece – the movement is more often to the left. The eye movement to the right, it is argued, suggests a greater use of the left hemisphere.

Brainedness and handedness

As already suggested, there is a definite relationship between handedness and the brain which is dominant for language. Nearly all right-handers process language primarily in the left brain as do somewhere between fifty and seventy per cent of non-right-handers.

There are many explanations for the connection between right-handedness and left-brainedness for speech. One of these makes the basic assumption that there is a slight tendency in man towards right-handedness. The right hand and left brain, therefore, would have been primarily involved in gestural communication. Thus the left brain had a communication bias. Later, language started to take over from gesture. By this time the left brain's superiority for communication had been established.

Other writers have however suggested that right-handedness is the result of speech having originally been located in the left brain. Some researchers have pointed to the similarities between the complex motor movements of the hand and of the vocal cords. They argue therefore that it is not surprising that one hemisphere, usually the left, took on these specialised movements – the hand movements and the fine movements of the vocal cords.

Recent research suggests that there may be an anatomical basis for the left-brain language specialisation. One study suggests that about seventy per cent of the population have a slightly larger 'planum temporale' (part of the area of the brain concerned with language) in the left hemisphere. It is interesting to note that about thirty per cent of the population is not strongly right-handed.

Various non-environmental explanations have been put forward to explain handedness, or brainedness, or both. Corballis and Beale give an excellent summary of the biological background, and argue 'that handedness and cerebral lateralization are indeed for the most part predetermined at birth, ... [and] that symmetry and asymmetries, including those of hand and brain, are not coded directly in the genes, although they may be subject to indirect genetic influences. Rather, they depend on information that is coded in the cytoplasm of the oocyte, the cell in the mother that undergoes meiosis to form the ovum.' They conclude 'that right-handedness and the left-cerebral representation of speech are expressions of a fundamental left-right gradient that is ultimately cytoplasmic rather than genetic.' They conclude that 'some people inherit a lack of any consistent genetic disposition toward manual or cerebral asymmetry. Among this minority, handedness and cerebral lateralization are determined at random, and possibly independently.'

There seems to be a difference between left-handers who come from a left-handed family and those who come from a right-handed family. A left-hander with a history of left-handedness in the family may have speech and visual abilities present in both hemispheres. On the other hand (!) left-handers without any history of left-handedness in the family tend to have the same brain organisation as right-handers – that is, with speech in the left hemisphere. This difference is one reason why many researchers argue that there must be a genetic basis for handedness and 'brainedness'. For example, a left-handed individual who has a history of left-handedness in the family is often better at recovering speech following damage to either the left or right hemisphere. This is as expected as speech in these cases may be present in the left and right hemisphere. However, damage to the left hemisphere of a person who is left-handed without a history of left-handedness in the family usually results in long term damage to speech ability. 'It is reasonable to argue for a genetic basis for such mechanisms, as opposed to an environmental determination, since an environmental influence that affects cerebral organisation for the familial left-handed and not the nonfamilial seems highly improbable at best.'*

Finally, left-handed mothers have been seen to have a slightly greater chance of having left-handed children than do fathers who are left-handed. This suggests that there is probably a slight genetic influence being passed down by the mother in favour of left-handedness.

Male and female

Males have shown themselves to be slightly better at performing visual tasks than females. Females, on the other hand, tend to score slightly better than males on verbal fluency tests. It has been noticed that the left brain in females tends to specialise for language earlier than in males.**

One fascinating explanation for this male superiority in spatial tasks is explained as follows by one researcher: 'Most of human evolution must have taken place under conditions where for the male hunting members of society accurate information about both the immediate and distant environment was of paramount importance.'†

There is an interesting connection between right and maleness, left and femaleness. Parmenides suggested that the sex of the embryo would be male if it were on the right side and female if it were on the left side. Anoxoras suggested that the father was always responsible for the sex of a child. If the seed

---

* *Psychological Bulletin* Vol 84 No 3, May 1977

** Buffery and Gray 'Sex Differences in the Development of Spatial and Linguistic Skills' in *Gender Differences: Their Ontogeny and Significance* (ed Ounsted and Taylor)

† D. Kimura in *Scientific American* March 1973

came from the right testis it would produce a boy, and if from the left the result would be a girl. In fact this theory gave rise to a practice of attempting to pre-determine a child's sex. If parents wanted a male child, the father would be recommended to fasten a kind of tourniquet around the left testis, and vice versa.

The association between left and female, right and male, has reappeared in research on the embryo. 'It is not the side of the father or the mother which determines the sex of the embryo, as the Greeks thought, but the embryo itself shows some degree of lateralisation with regard to its actual potentialities. Although normally the potentialities are safely overridden by the sex chromosomes constitution, the idea of an association between right and male, left and female is basically correct.'*

The same article also refers to some research on fingerprints, which suggests that there are definite differences between the right and left hands during the fourth month of the foetus's development. Usually the ridge-count of the right hand is more than that of the left. 'Thus there appears to be some degree of asymmetry favouring the right hand already in the foetus.'

The football (table tennis) machine mystery

Many a public house has a game whereby you have an equivalent to a television screen on which you can play electronic football, or table tennis, right through to more exotic aircraft fights. There are kits available which enable you to use your television screen for the same purpose. When I have played these games I have always presumed that there would be an advantage to play on the left hand side as the control knob is more immediately available to the right hand (I am right-handed). However, this does not necessarily seem to be the case.

* *New Scientist* 13 January 1977

Two Brains

In January 1978 *New Scientist* carried a letter by Andrew J. Prior, aged 14. He was writing to say that he had noticed a definite advantage to the player that was defending the right of the screen. To make sure that this was not simply a defect in the controls, he had tried inverting the screen so that the other player had the other control, and he noticed that the player on the right still seemed to have the advantage. He tentatively put forward the suggestion that the player was more used to 'some left to right' scanning – for example, as in reading.

Rather like the mystery of the left-handed whelk, this issue caught many people's interest. The idea that we might be better at 'from left to right' scanning is based on the idea that our training for reading is left to right. A later correspondent made the point that it would be interesting to see if the Chinese who write from top to bottom, also find this effect.

Another suggestion was that where you have two right-handed players, the ball arrives at the 'forehand' for the player defending the right screen and the 'backhand' of the player that is defending the left. For most players this would again suggest that the right side is preferable.

Another correspondent, who seemed to be particularly well informed about such football machines in public houses, remarked that he had noticed that pub sets often provided a slightly better frontal view for the right-hander.

Suddenly the whole issue took on larger proportions. Dr Stuart Butler noted that the 'advantage in defending the right-hand goal while playing TV games is probably a manifestation of the brain's functional asymmetry; in particular of the special skill of its right hemisphere in processing visuospatial information'.

The square below illustrates the layout of a typical TV football machine screen. A and B represent the two goals. If you look at point B the screen will be largely in your left visual field, which in turn is registered on the right of the retina which in turn is largely wired up to the right hemisphere. The case is reversed if you look at A. This means that the player on the right has the best link up with the visuospatial thinking area of the brain.

Stuart Butler also noticed that the player on the right (I am presuming that all players are right-handed in this study) played better when he operated the control with his left hand. Recall that the left hand is controlled by the right hemisphere. It was noticed that the left hand was better when the player was looking at goal A or goal B.

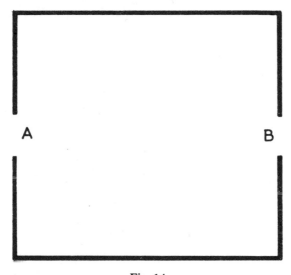

Fig. 14

However, the advantage of the left hand disappeared when the player was looking straight at the screen. 'The expected superiority of the right hand in controlling the ball appeared only when the subjects were looking directly at the moving stimuli . . .' With a player generally looking at the centre of the screen information is being fed from the left and right fields and so to both hemispheres. As Dr Butler points out: 'Potentially, conflicting control signals could be generated under this condition, for relay directly or indirectly to motor systems and this is something the well-engineered brain would presumably be designed to avoid. We are tempted to speculate that some old-fashioned dominance of the left hemisphere over motor control is the answer. The biological advantage of avoiding conflicting commands would outweigh the disadvantage of assigning control to a hemisphere which is not always the best one for the job.' In a personal communication Dr Butler points out that the specialisation of the hemispheres can be seen as very useful for 'higher cerebral functions'. However, this specialisation is not so useful for simpler tasks, as in this case of the TV game.

Andrew Prior's original letter gives rise to two points. Firstly, those people with this visuospatial ability in their right hemisphere, that is practically all right-handers and around half of left-handers, are advised when playing television football and similar games to take the right hand control knob! Secondly, the stronger visuospatial awareness for information in the left visual field obviously has important implications for the layout of visual apparatus in display units in aircrafts, cars and elsewhere.

Why different brains?

What was the evolutionary purpose of the specialisation of the two brains? Robert Ornstein suggests that the left-brain thinking had definite survival value: 'the analytic mode in which there is a separation of objects, of the self from others . . . has proved useful in individual biological survival.'* The left brain's high-level language ability has also had social importance. The spatial awareness of the right brain was important in dealing with the environment and its dangers:

---

* R. H. Ornstein *The Psychology of Consciousness*

"The last applicant suggested that on the one hand I could do this or on the other hand I could do that. Let's see what you have to say."

The evidence would, accordingly, strongly suggest that the abrupt evolutionary change from the functionally symmetric hemispheres of the ape to the profoundly asymmetric hemispheres of man is correlated with the discontinuity from mute to speaking animals. Those ancient ape-men who possessed both brain bisymmetry and language, but did not possess the ability to see a hungry lion embedded like a hidden figure in the tall savannah grass, paid for their speech with their lives. Their cousins, also possessing language, and, in addition, a mute, Gestalt-synthesizing, figure-ground-separating, hemisphere, saw the lions, escaped, and, for good or ill, fathered the race of Man. Why are the left-handers still with us? Evolutionary law demands that any genotype which survives, if it is inferior in some way to others, must, by virtue of its survival, be superior in another way.*

* J. Levy in *Hemispheric Disconnection and Cerebral Function* (ed M. Kinsbourne and W. L. Smith)

Fig. 15

Levy asked one of his young split-brain patients to draw a man. 'His production . . . has the right side visualising a girl and the left conceptualising her name', thus epitomising the difference between the two halves of the brain (Fig. 15).

THE TWO-SIDED MAN

Rudyard Kipling

Much I owe to the Lands that grew —
More to the lives that fed —
But most to the Allah Who gave me two
Separate sides to my head.

Much I left on the Good and the True
In the faiths beneath the sun
But most upon Allah Who gave me two
Sides to my head, not one.

I would go without shirt or shoe,
Friend, tobacco or bread,
Sooner than lose for a minute the two
Separate sides of my head!

3 Two Worlds

The symbolism of left and right — Artist versus scientist — Thought and language — Education — Learning — Specialisation — Getting through — Problem solving — Four-stage problem-solving approach — Creativity — Religion and mysticism — Are opposites opposite? — The individual and society

The symbolism of left and right

In *The Psychology of Consciousness*, Robert Ornstein asks his readers to consider the following questions about their left and right sides: 'Which side of you is more feminine? Which is more masculine? Which side do you consider the "dark" side of yourself? Which side is the "lighter"? Which side is more active? ... more passive? ... more logical? ... more "intuitive"? ... more mysterious? ... more artistic?'

More often than not the left hand has been associated with intuition and the artistic, while the right hand is more often associated with logic, order and reason. There appears, therefore, to be some relationship between the symbolism of the left hand and the function of the right brain, and between the symbolism of the right hand and the functions of the left brain. It is fascinating to speculate how man developed a symbolism of left and right that seems to reflect the nature and structure of the brain:

> Since childhood, I have been enchanted by the fact and the symbolism of the right hand and the left – the one the doer, the other the dreamer. The right is order and lawfulness, *le droit*. Its beauties are those of geometry and taut implication. Reaching for knowledge with the right hand is science. Yet to say only that much of science is to overlook one of its excitements, for the great hypotheses of sciences are gifts carried in the left hand.
>
> Of the left hand we say that it is awkward and, while it has been proposed that art students can seduce their proper hand to more expressiveness by drawing first with the left, we nonetheless suspect this function. The French speak of the illegitimate descendant as being *à main gauche*, and, though the heart is virtually at the centre of the thoracic

cavity, we listen for it on the left. Sentiment, intuition, bastardy. And should we say that reaching for knowledge with the left hand is art? Again it is not enough, for as surely as the recital of a daydream differs from the well-wrought tale, there is a barrier between undisciplined fantasy and art. To climb the barrier requires a right hand adept at technique and artifice.

And so I have argued . . . that the scientist and the poet do not live at antipodes, and I urge . . . that the artificial separation of the two modes of knowing cripples the contemporary intellectual . . .*

The two modes of knowing are described by the great physicist Oppenheimer:

These two ways of thinking, the way of time and history, and the way of eternity and timelessness, are both part of man's effort to comprehend the world in which he lives. Neither is comprehended in the other nor reducible to it . . . each supplementing the other, neither telling the whole story.

Much has been written about the symbolism of the left and right hands. Although it bears some relationship to the nature of the brain, it would be very misleading to presume that the symbolism of the hands provides an accurate description of brain function. There is a risk that the research on the two brains will be interpreted too loosely. As mentioned earlier, it can be practically impossible to say that one type of ability resides solely in one brain or hemisphere. Furthermore, in the case of certain left-handers, the whole brain organisation seems to be different. Even in right-handers, according to recent research, brain organisation may vary from individual to individual. It is important to see mental abilities within the context of the entire brain. The divisions that can be made

* J. S. Bruner *On Knowing*

within the brain are practically infinite, and to talk about the brain solely in terms of right and left hemispheres is ultimately going to give a misleading picture. The brain is a totally integrated organ and finally needs to be considered as such.

In the rest of this book the expressions 'rightism' and 'rightist' will be used to refer to the general mental abilities of the right hemisphere and all the symbolism of the left hand. The words 'leftism' or 'leftist' will be used to refer to the symbolism of the right hand and the function of the left brain, thus shifting the emphasis from the symbolism attached to the hand to the function of the brain that controls that hand. Rightism includes such areas as visual awareness, intuitive thinking, dreams and daydreams, and thinking of the insight ('Eureka!'), holistic (whole grasp), sensuous, 'soft' and largely non-verbal kinds. Within leftism are included verbal, analytical, logical, abstract, theoretical and time-orientated thinking.

Artist versus scientist

C. P. Snow popularised the notion of two opposing cultures — scientists versus humanists — in *The Two Cultures: and A Second Look*. Snow argued that these cultures had great difficulty in even beginning to try to talk to each other:

> Persons educated with the greatest intensity we know can no longer communicate with each other on the plane of their major intellectual concern. This is serious for our creative, intellectual and, above all, our normal life . . . It is dangerous to have two cultures which can't and don't communicate. In a time when science is determining much of our destiny, that is, whether we live or die, it is dangerous in the most practical terms.

Snow argues that to ask a question like 'What is mass or acceleration?' would be a fairly alien consideration for nine out of ten people. He goes on to point out that this is the scientific equivalent of saying 'Can you read?' 'So the great edifice of modern physics goes up, and the majority of the cleverest people in the western world have about as much insight into it as their neolithic ancestors would have had.' Snow's remedy for this problem lies with education. The need for an education which is both scientific and artistic is a worthy goal, but more important, many argue, is the need to develop and harmonise the underlying mental processes.

The psychologist, J. S. Bruner, is 'a little out of patience with the alleged split between "the two cultures" for the two are not simply external ways of life, one pursued by humanists, the other by scientists. They are ways of living with one's own experience.' What is needed is 'not an institutionalised cultural bridge outside, but an internal transfer from left to right . . .'

Recently, a new split between two cultures has been suggested. The two cultures this time are business and academia. One recent survey found that executives 'tend to use right-brain processes even in supposedly analytical tasks, whereas operations researchers (PhDs on university faculties) use the "appropriate" hemisphere for the tasks. For many years the field of management science has noted that top-level executives – who seem to operate intuitively – pay little or no attention to complex mathematical problem-solving models created by operations researchers.'*

Thought and Language

How far are non-verbal, intuitive and pictorial types of thinking involved in scientific breakthrough? Arthur Koestler, in *The Ghost in the Machine*, says: 'There is a popular superstition, according to which scientists arrive at their discoveries by reasoning in strictly rational, precise, verbal terms. The evidence indicates that they do nothing of the sort.'

* *Psychophysiology* 14, 385–92. Quotation from *Brain Mind Bulletin* Vol 2 No 18, Aug 1977

A nationwide inquiry was carried out in 1945 in America to establish what sort of methods top mathematicians employed in working. The results show that, with only two exceptions, they thought neither in verbal terms, nor in algebraic symbols, but relied on visual imagery of a vague, hazy kind. Einstein was among those who answered the questionnaire; he wrote:

> The words or the language, as they are written or spoken, do not seem to play any role in my mechanism of thought. The physical entities which seem to serve as elements in thought are certain signs and more or less clear images which can be 'voluntarily' reproduced and combined . . .
> The above-mentioned elements are, in any case, of visual and some of muscular types. Conventional words or other signs have to be sought for laboriously only in a secondary stage, when the mentioned associative play is sufficiently established and can be reproduced at will.*

In fact in one letter Einstein wrote: 'I am untidy and a daydreamer.' However, this daydreamer had the ability to turn his images into very concrete theories. Albert Einstein is said to have discovered the theory of relativity by picturing himself riding on a ray of light.**

It is interesting to consider how many people must have great insights and yet lack the basic language or mathematical tools to translate or convey their ideas. An intuitive hunch or an image is often found at the base of a scientific breakthrough, and on the other hand much more than daydreaming fancy is required for any artistic achievement – some analytical capacity is also necessary.

An often quoted example of rightist thinking in scientific discovery comes from the French chemist Kekulé. His revelation of the structure of the benzene ring is described:

---

* Quoted in Arthur Koestler *The Act of Creation*
** Mike Samuels and Nancy Samuels *Seeing with the Mind's Eye*

I turned my chair to the fire and dozed . . . Again the atoms were gambolling before my eyes. This time the small groups kept modestly in the background. My mental eye, rendered more acute by repeated visions of this kind, could now distinguish larger structures, of manifold conformation; long rows, sometimes more closely fitted together; all twining and twisting in snakelike motion. But look! What was that? One of the snakes had seized hold of its own tail, and the form whirled mockingly before my eyes. As if by a flash of lightning I awoke . . .*

The discovery which came from this visual insight has been referred to as 'the most brilliant piece of prediction to be found in the whole range of organic chemistry'.

The discoverer of Fuchsian functions, Henri Poincaré, described himself thus: 'Every day I seated myself at my work table, stayed an hour or two, tried a great number of combinations and reached no results. One evening, contrary to my custom, I drank black coffee and could not sleep. Ideas rose in clouds; I felt them collide until pairs interlocked, so to speak, making a stable combination. By the next morning . . . I had only to write out the results, which took but a few hours.'**

The strong visualising ability of the scientist seems to be a very great asset. The technological innovator Tesla (inventor of the AC generator and fluorescent lighting) is described as being able to 'project before his eyes a picture complete in every detail, of every part of the machine. These pictures were more vivid than any blueprint.'† Apparently Tesla was also able to leave the machinery running in his mind and so keep an eye open for any possible signs of wear and tear.

Although high-level mathematical, analytical and verbal ability is seen to be necessary to follow through these original

---

* Quoted in Arthur Koestler *The Act of Creation*
** B. Ghiselin *The Creative Process*
† J. J. O'Neill *Progidal Genius: The Life of Nikola Tesla*

insights and intuitions, language in the first place can impede the scientific discovery. Language can limit perception — according to what is known as the Whorfian hypothesis, man's perception is greatly influenced by the language he uses. The Whorfian hypothesis was formulated before modern research fully revealed the differing natures and functions of the two halves of the brain. The right brain, which seems to be very independent of language, may be little affected by the limitations of language structures, and the Whorfian hypothesis may be more applicable to the kinds of thought typical of the left hemisphere.

The idea underlying the Whorfian hypothesis can be extended to suggest that not only may language limit our perception, it also limits the intensity with which we can experience our surroundings. Various writers and thinkers have suggested that there are realms of experience or of mental awareness beyond the sphere of language. Wordsworth believed that 'often we have to get away from speech in order to think clearly'. For Koestler, 'language can become a screen which stands between the thinker and reality. This is the reason why true creativity often starts where language ends.'* Huxley expresses a similar idea even more forcibly:

> Every individual is at once the beneficiary and the victim of the linguistic tradition into which he has been born — the beneficiary inasmuch as language gives access to the accumulated record of other people's experience, the victim in so far as it confirms him in the belief that reduced awareness is the only awareness and as it bedevils his sense of reality, so that he is all too apt to take his concepts for data, his words for actual things.**

An artist, then, needs to combine leftist and rightist thinking if he is to harness his creative spirit, while the scientist needs to

---

* Arthur Koestler *The Act of Creation*
** Aldous Huxley *The Doors of Perception*

be able to use rightist thinking as a source of inspiration. Maslow, a very positive and humanistic psychologist, has described two kinds of creativity, primary and secondary. Primary creativity he describes as 'creativeness which comes out of the unconscious, and which is the source of new discovery (or real novelty) of ideas which depart from what exists at this point'. Secondary creativity is 'a technique whereby uncreative people can create and discover, by working along with a lot of other people, by standing upon the shoulders of people who have come before them, by being cautious and careful, and so on. That I'll call secondary creativeness and secondary science.'*

It seems as if all great scientists have relied heavily on this process of primary creativity, which is essentially a blend of rightist and leftist thought. Artists as well – Leonardo da Vinci – used both mental styles to the full. In an increasingly complex world, with rapid technological change and, if one agrees with C. P. Snow, an almost insurmountable barrier between scientists and humanists, and between different academic disciplines, we need an educational system which will encourage people to develop both leftist and rightist thinking for themselves.

Education

For many children, education involves the development of certain abilities to the detriment of the more imaginative and creative abilities. The 'adult' world is generally more verbal and more categorised than that of the child, and although education must to an extent involve 'acclimatising' children to the 'adult' world, it is not surprising that that world may seem barren to them, and that they lose some of their enthusiasm for learning.

* J. L. Adams *Conceptual Blockbusting*

Ornstein suggests that middle-class children develop a more verbal/analytical way of thinking, while working-class children develop a more visual/gestalt way of thinking. He goes on to argue that American education is therefore biased against the working class. There continues today a very definite bias against the more creative subjects – crafts, music, dancing, etc. The linguistic and mathematical (leftist) subjects are still considered superior. The same trend is seen in the financial and class status rewards we give socially – for example, the difference in status between an academic and a craftsman. Maximum prestige is often given to non-applied subjects. In university circles (certainly in the past and to an extent probably today), a non-applied subject may implicitly be considered superior to an applied subject. A theoretical subject – for example, philosophy – will often carry greater prestige than engineering.

One reason why the craft-orientated subjects have in the past been considered inferior to more 'leftist' subjects may be that originally such leftist skills as reading and writing and studying ancient languages were the preserve of an elite – the clergy, lawyers, administrators, gentlemen and so on – and that these subjects are as a result still felt in some way to be superior.

The three basic skills of reading, writing and arithmetic all involve leftist thinking. For some reason some educationalists seem to think that it is only possible to develop *either* leftist skills *or* rightist skills, and the present debate about teaching methods and the curriculum tends to polarise teachers into those advocating a return to more traditional methods and subjects and those arguing for a more progressive curriculum and more progressive methods. Certainly education should teach the basic (leftist) skills; and it should also seek to enhance the individual's creative potential.

Educators recognise that school very often presents a barren image to a child's fertile mind. One of the advantages of the newer teaching methods is that they encourage teachers to talk in the children's terms, and one of the reasons for the success of 'experimental' and 'discovery' learning methods is that information may be less 'taught' and encourage children to become involved in living-out real situations.

Another way in which modern teaching methods are breaking down one of the strongholds of 'leftist' educational method is by teaching across the divisions between 'subjects'. Areas of knowledge naturally overlap and complement each other and rightist educational theory tends to prefer more integrated and interrelated methods of teaching.

Babies and young children nearly always seem to exhibit interest or curiosity. If the teacher can direct the child's interests, his horizons will widen and this will generate new interest. This wider interest cannot be satisfied if the teacher does not have a wide and integrated scope of knowledge, and can not see the natural ebb and flow of one subject into all others.

There are some interesting signs of schools trying to incorporate more rightist thinking into their curriculum. One art centred programme for 'elementary schoolers resulted in a general decline during the first year or two, then steady gains until the youngsters had surpassed the norms. Schools reported improved attendance as well.'*

Not only is it important to incorporate more rightist thinking, in certain skills certain research suggests that leftist thinking can, in fact, interfere with effective performance. An American art teacher, Betty Edwards, believes that artistic performance can be improved by reducing left brain interference. In her teaching she tries to enhance the right hemisphere's spatial ability and reduce reliance upon more analytical perception. She points out: 'Many of these tricks had been known by artists all along, but there hadn't been a

* *Brain Mind Bulletin* Vol 2 No 22

conceptual framework to explain why they work.'* Such techniques include drawing upside down portraits – the idea here is that the left brain gives up as the student is forced to try and draw what he actually sees as opposed to what he expects to be in the picture. Awareness of the space around an object is argued to be as important as the object itself.

Learning

After concentrating for hour after hour on tasks involving the use of leftist thinking, many people find that more creative, daydreaming, rightist thinking tends to get in the way. They may become over-aware of their surroundings, of noises, and may become restless, or start daydreaming. It is almost as though the right brain feels left out. This may help to explain why some people, when learning, like to doodle or listen to music – both activities involving the right hemisphere.

Dimond and Beaumont suggest that 'If the brain has two or more systems at work in perception, it could offset fatigue by distribution of perceptual load between the cerebral hemispheres, just as a heavy suitcase passed backwards and forwards between the arms.'**

If you are involved in leftist thinking, studying or listening to a talk, this creative rightist thinking can be a major hindrance. There are several ways that you can incorporate the more rightist, daydreaming type of thinking so as not to interfere with leftist thinking and in many cases to complement that leftist thinking. These are as follows:

Notes When taking notes, try to incorporate rightist thinking by using colourful, imagistic, patterned notes. One way is to take notes in the form of a 'mind pattern' or 'map' (Fig. 11), according to the following principles:

---

* *Brain Mind Bulletin* Vol 3 No 3
** S. J. Dimond and G. J. Beaumont *Hemisphere Function in the Human Brain*

1   The title is written in the middle of a plain piece of paper.

2   The main points radiate from the centre. Try to use single words. The next most important points are linked to the main points, and in this way a tree-like structure grows as information is added.

3   It is usually clearer if the individual words are written on the line.

4   Use arrows, codes and colours to help to relate and link up the various ideas.

5   Use images or symbols if you feel these represent more immediately the way you are thinking.

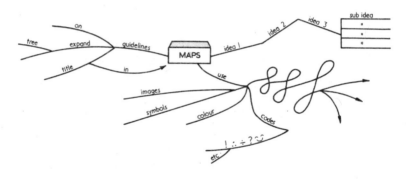

Fig. 16

One major rightist advantage of the map form of note-taking is that a large body of information can be represented or recorded on a small visual area. This naturally helps the rightist overall grasp of an area of information.

The same patterning or mapping approach can be used to stimulate thinking. With the most important ideas going nearest the centre, simply map out the ideas as they occur. Fit in each idea where it seems most appropriate. As before, the most important ideas are nearest the centre, and the more incidental ideas towards the outside of the pattern or map.

When thinking in an orderly, logical fashion, one tends to reduce the possibility of coming up with a more original or creative idea. By trying to go beyond the more limiting structures of logic and grammar and using this single-word mapping system, one very often establishes new ideas and perspectives.

In using this type of creative map, try to jot down the ideas as quickly as they come up. Very often the ideas will occur in a seemingly random way. This type of creative exercise relies upon association − sometimes logical but very often not. Having thrown up all the possible ideas, the map can then be structured by imposing some form of numbering upon it.

One useful technique for generating more information is to use the questions so often asked by children − who? how? when? where? why? what? It is interesting to note that adults use these questions much less than children. Some people might argue that this is because adults know it all! More probably it is because adults are less willing than children to show that they do not know about something.

The questions are used as follows. For example, ask the question 'What?' of the centre. By asking 'What?' you may come up with the idea for a definition. Then try the question 'When?' then 'Where?', etc. Having asked all the questions of the centre, start asking each question of the next main branches, and then the sub-branches, then the sub-sub-branches, etc. By doing this, you find that you generate more and more information. Through relying upon less logical, more rightist thinking, you very often find that you come up with ideas and information that you did not realise you had. Also you may put the information in a new perspective (Fig. 16).

Imagination Greater use of imagination, ie rightist thinking, can also be used in what would normally be considered a leftist

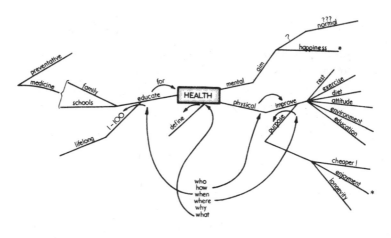

Fig. 17

thinking task. This can be done by 'living through' the situation being described, by identifying with the characters – for example, putting yourself in the position of the research scientist. These are ways of making the information more real, more colourful, more imagistic, and incidentally, more memorable.

Another way to harness the imagination in leftist learning (and incidentally also to help to develop more rightist thinking) is by using mnemonics. The Greeks are originally credited with the development of these highly effective systems of remembering. When devising mnemonics, use *linked, outstanding* images. In using this system you create as concrete an image as possible, and then link this image to another image. Make the links and the images as 'outstanding' as possible.

A simple example of this system could be devised to help one remember the following three objects – coffee, butter, shoes. First, link coffee to butter. For this you can simply imagine splitting a coffee bean to find inside a large slab of butter. Then create a link between butter and shoes. Imagine taking some butter and taking the sole of your shoe, and buttering the sole so as to make a sandwich. You find that if you think of coffee you will think of butter and then shoes. In fact you can carry on linking the objects in this way so as to remember hundreds of objects. This type of highly creative thinking can be very useful in remembering names, dates and even new vocabulary.*

Breaks During learning, take breaks. These allow for a rest from leftist thinking and also an opportunity for more relaxed, more rightist thinking – for example, gazing, relaxing, doodling, listening to music, etc. As a general guideline, breaks every twenty to forty minutes can greatly help concentration. After thirty minutes take a break for just two or three minutes and then start the next thirty-minute period. After two hours a longer break is recommended.

It is often during these breaks that the useful insight or 'eureka' experience occurs. It is almost as though leftist information is taken in, slowly digested and considered by rightist thinking which in turn will feed its message back to the more verbal thinking. The adage 'all work and no play makes Jack a dull boy' seems very apt in describing what happens if we use leftist thinking non-stop. If one asks people when and where they very often have their best ideas, replies will probably include: while driving, shaving, gardening, on holiday, in the bath, on the loo, in bed just before going to sleep, on waking up, staring vacantly, etc – all times when leftist thinking is reduced, rightist increased. For example, Mozart is renowned to have said that many of his ideas would appear while travelling or walking.

Breaks are useful for coming up with new ideas, but it would be misleading to presume that constant relaxed imagistic rightist thinking would provide a constant source of new ideas. Rightist creative thinking seems best at throwing out new and original ideas but only if leftist thinking has also been used.

* M. E. Brown *Memory Matters*

Charles Darwin describes well the great loss that can occur if thinking and experience is too much of one type:

> Up to the age of thirty or beyond it, poetry of many kinds ... gave me great pleasure, and even as a schoolboy I took intense delight in Shakespeare, especially in the historical plays. I have also said that formerly pictures gave me considerable, and music very great, delight. But now for many years I cannot endure to read a line of poetry: I have tried lately to read Shakespeare, and found it so intolerably dull that it nauseated me. I have also lost almost any taste for pictures or music ... My mind seems to have become a kind of machine for grinding general laws out of large collections of fact, but why this should have caused the atrophy of that part of the brain alone, on which the higher tastes depend, I cannot conceive ... The loss of these tastes is a loss of happiness and may possibly be injurious to the intellect, and more probably to the moral character, by enfeebling the emotional part of our nature.*

Specialisation

Another major implication of this leftist/rightist argument is that practically everyone has the ability (and the need) to develop a more scientific *and* a more creative/artistic type of thinking. 'The men who teach him [the young scientist] science will encourage him to ignore the warm sprawl of emotion in which arts men wallow, and to reason with complete impersonality. Conversely, those who teach the budding arts specialist may reassure him (as he had long suspected) that scientists are narrow and philistine, and that all the paraphernalia of mathematics and logic is unnecessary to the conduct of a civilised life. Both arts and science teaching look like systems of cultural indoctrination and it would be odd if they had no effect.'**

---

* From an autobiography of Charles Darwin (ed Norah Barlow, Collins 1958)
** Liam Hudson *Contrary Imaginations*

Educational systems channel people into scientific or artistic directions comparatively early on in their lives. This can aggravate the gulf between 'the two cultures'. In the same way that a great scientific or artistic breakthrough often involves the use of leftist and rightist thinking, so children should be trained to use these two complementary approaches. Craft subjects, art, musical appreciation, dance and movement classes are now held in higher esteem, but the progressive approach to education has at times been wrongly associated with the supposed decline in basic literacy and numeracy. If greater attention should be paid to basic leftist skills, an increased attention to rightist thinking is also necessary.

Colin Blakemore has pointed out that the 'special mental territories of the minor, right hemisphere – spatial perception, pictorial recognition and intuitive thought – are not easily amenable to conventional education, nor is it clear that they would benefit from years of formal instruction.'*

Whereas leftist thinking – language, logic, mathematical ability – can be taught to some extent, the less verbal abilities of rightist thinking can be developed through participation in music, crafts, etc. Some educationists today argue that we concentrate too much on knowledge as opposed to skills or competences. What is important for a child is to be able to make appropriate decisions and solve problems in the outside world, (as opposed to knowing all about the wives of Henry VIII). Therefore, various styles of thinking need to be developed. A major division in these styles can be leftist and rightist. Specific examples of styles include: analytical, mathematical, linguistic, aesthetic, moral and intuitive.

One further educational implication of the specialisation of the two brains is the use of 'biofeedback training' to try to turn on the appropriate thinking. Electroencephalograms (EEGs) can be used to try to establish which type of thinking is

---

* C. Blakemore *The Mechanics of the Mind*

dominant in an individual – to find out if an individual tends more towards pictorial or verbal thinking etc and also to encourage the thinking style to suit the learning task.

Getting through

Imagine a child who has spent a day in the midst of a thick forest, playing with his friends. He arrives home in the evening and his parents ask about the day he has had. For the child the experience is very 'real' – in the sense that his experience was very immediate and free of the catagorisation of words and ideas, etc. The child may have difficulty explaining about his day to his parents for two reasons. Firstly, his language ability is not as developed as that of his parents and secondly the inadequacy and the inappropriateness of language reduces the realness of his experience.

Many parents talk to their children in simple and especially concrete terms – otherwise a child may have difficulty in grasping an adult's meaning. Children also tend to appreciate greater use of gesture, voice inflection and changes in volume. Children like and understand rightist thinking.

Imagine a person looking at a house he has just built – called 'The Stables'. The house is what the man is experiencing – the name 'The Stables' or the word 'house' refer to the object but are in fact not the object itself. The owner can think of the house in a more general way, that is at a higher level of abstraction. He can think of it, for example, as a building. He can go even to a higher level and think of the house as a possession. As he goes further up the scale of abstraction, he uses a word which includes many more possible objects. Abstraction is a leftist type of thinking.

A higher level of abstraction is rather like a larger umbrella above a smaller umbrella. Certain professionals, professions and experts are accused of being over-specialist in their language. They may also be very fluent in the use and understanding of their particular levels of abstraction. The danger of this can be compared to ageing – it comes on very slowly and in the end is very difficult to get rid of! It can take a long time to master a specialist language. During this process the individual can become the victim as opposed to the controller of the expert terms and levels of abstraction.

Many people consider that the hallmark of a person who really knows his particular subject is that he can express himself quite clearly even in the simplest of terms. In other words, he has mastered the expert language of his subject and can also stand outside that language so as to re-express technical ideas in simpler, often solid, terms. This reminds me of the story about Edith Piaf's arrival in America. On leaving the plane she was surrounded by journalists. They asked who she would most like to meet. Her reply was 'Einstein'. She maintained that she grasped practically everything that Einstein put forward. He was presumably a person able to assess another person's knowledge and therefore use the appropriate vocabulary and analogies to help their understanding. They met. Piaf had always found reading difficult as she had an eye weakness from childhood, however, she apparently kept some work of Einstein by her bedside for the remainder of her life.

The general public have grown suspicious of some areas of expertise. Many people are surprised how simple many of the concepts in law, in psychology, in sociology become when explained by somebody who can communicate the ideas clearly. The expression 'bullshit baffles brains' illustrates this suspicion. A higher level of abstraction is a very useful method of obtaining a bird's eye view and talking in shorthand. Problems occur, however, where the specialist is trying to explain the idea to the public. Subjects like philosophy, psychology, sociology and economics apply to everyday people. The ideas within these subjects are relevant to day-to-day living. In communicating these ideas greater understanding is often attained if a lower level of abstraction is used.

Right at the bottom of the scale of abstraction is the thing itself as perceived. Leftist thinking labels and abstracts while rightist thinking perceives and appreciates the object more immediately. Language at a low level of abstraction which uses real situations, real images, analogies, metaphors and similes usually makes for a clearer and more memorable explanation. An idea expressed in language full of images lives on in the mind, whereas an idea couched in abstract terms, no matter how impressive it may seem at first, may subsequently fade and be forgotten.

The effectiveness of imagery is one reason why many religious teachers have used parables and stories to convey their ideas. Parables have the advantage that they may be remembered as stories even if the underlying ideas are not properly understood, and long after they have been told their inner meaning may suddenly become apparent. Ideas less vividly expressed are not likely to remain dormant in the mind in this way.

Problem-solving

James Adams argues that there is a cultural block that goes as follows: 'Reason, logic, numbers, utility, practicality are *good*; feeling, intuition, qualitative judgement, pleasure are *bad*.' He suggests that in problem-solving we make good use of our leftist thinking but leave out rightist thinking almost altogether. 'This block against emotion, feeling, pleasure stems from our puritan heritage and our technology-based culture.'* He also argues that there is a bias against more 'feminine' mental activities. Whereas the female has been thought of as more sensitive and intuitive, the male historically has been trained to

---

* J. L. Adams *Conceptual Blockbusting*

be practical and logical. In problem-solving and most mental and physical activity there is a place for all of these traits.

Problem-solving ability in most people can be improved by developing leftist and rightist thinking. In many people leftist (analytical, logical, verbal) thinking is well developed, and therefore it is the rightist thinking that needs to be developed. This more imaginative thinking can be enhanced by attempting to improve visual powers by training oneself to observe details more carefully. Drawing also helps to increase visual awareness.

Four-stage problem-solving approach

The following four stages provide an approach to problem-solving and decision-making which encourages the use of both leftist and rightist thinking. This approach presumes that you are not having to make a 'snap' decision or give an immediate solution – you at least have a few minutes.

Stage 1 Establish clearly what the problem is. It often helps to record what the problem is by using words and/or images, perhaps using a creative map. At this stage do not analyse what the problem is. Simply jot down all the ideas that come into your mind, again relying upon more associative, less logical (ie rightist) thinking. If the problem involves something solid like a mechanical process, draw it out so that you can see it.

Stage 2 At this stage jot down *all* possible solutions to the problem. In problem solving, people may often choose the first or second solution, either because it naturally comes to mind or because it seems to solve the problem. Instead, look for as many solutions as possible. Do not analyse the solutions. Accept what you might logically think to be ridiculous or absurd solutions. Try and reduce the role of the intellect at this stage:

Apparently it is not good – and indeed it hinders the creative work of the mind – if the intellect examines too closely the ideas already pouring in, as it were, at the gates. Regarded in isolation, an idea may be quite insignificant, and venturesome in the extreme, but it may acquire importance from an idea which follows it; perhaps, in a certain collocation with other ideas, which may seem equally absurd, it may be capable of furnishing a very serviceable link.*

The problem being solved may require a unique solution. Logical thinking, leftist thinking, is predominantly going to throw up various solutions or decisions that have been arrived at before. If the solution needs to be unique, rightist thinking needs to be used to obtain the intuitive insight and/or to throw out the new imaginative idea. Therefore, accept all crazy and ridiculous ideas.

Stage 3   At this stage take each solution in turn and see how it best solves all the aspects of the problem as stated or illustrated in Stage 1. A combination of two or more of the suggested solutions may in fact provide a better solution. Finally choose your best solution or solutions. Here leftist thinking and analysis are paramount.

Stage 4   Using both visual and/or logical types of thinking, try and see how the best solution could fail, with a view to seeing how your best solution could be improved.

To summarise, Stage 1 establishes the problem, Stage 2 gives as many solutions as possible, Stage 3 selects your best solution or solutions, Stage 4 decides how your best solution could fail with a view to further improvement. During all four stages you use leftist and rightist thinking as appropriate. Between each stage it can be a good idea to rest. The way that a rest period provides the 'eureka' insight has already been described.

* A statement by Schiller in *The Basic Writings of Sigmund Freud* (ed A. A. Bril)

Arthur Deikman has described two types of thinking, the 'action mode' and the 'receptive mode'. The action mode is logic- and language-orientated, the receptive mode is more sensitive and relaxed. The action mode is leftist, the receptive mode rightist. He describes a process in which there is:

> ... first a stage of directed intellectual attack on the problem leading to a feeling of impasse, then the stage of 'giving up', in which the person stops struggling with the problem and turns his attention to other things. During this unfocused rest period the solution to the problem manifests itself as an 'Aha' or 'Eureka' experience – the answer is suddenly there of itself. The final stage sees the return of directed intellectual activity as the 'answer' is worked over to assess its validity ... the first stage is one in which the action mode is used, followed by the receptive mode, in which the creative leap is made, followed by a return to the action mode to integrate the discovery.*

This idea of letting the more innate creative powers of the brain work on a problem is summarised in the phrase 'sleep on it'. The same effect can be noticed when trying to remember a name – to search consciously for it may only increase the delay in recall.

Bertrand Russell described himself as in effect 'sleeping on' books that he was about to write. He used to work intensively on preparing to write the book for a period of time and then to leave the work altogether – then to come back and to find that the book had written itself! This approach seems to work particularly well if there is a deadline to be met. A student writing an essay may find that if he researches his subject intensively and then writes immediately his ideas may come out in a rather unstructured way. However, to research the subject and then to write the essay several days later so as to meet a deadline very often produces a much better essay.

---

* 'Bimodal Consciousness' in *The Nature of Human Consciousness* (ed R. H. Ornstein)

Wherever possible, allow time for the mind to mull over problems and information. Often people come up with the useful insight and the automatic structuring of the information during such periods.

Creativity

The creative act involves the bringing together of two or more previously unrelated items, ideas or facts so as to come up with a new idea. Arthur Koestler in an essay on creativity defines the creative act 'as the combination of previously unrelated structures in such a way that you get more out of the emergent whole than you have put in'. He formulates the following creative categories – 'artistic originality', 'scientific discovery' and 'comic inspiration'. The first gives rise to the 'Ah' reaction, the second, that is scientific discovery, causes the 'Aha!', reaction and finally comic inspiration causes the 'Haha!' reaction.

J. S. Bruner argues that a creative act is one that produces 'effective surprise':

> I would propose that all of the forms of effective surprise grow out of combinatorial activity – a placing of things in new perspectives. But it is somehow not simply a taking of known elements and running them together by algorithm into a welter of permutations . . . to create consists precisely in not making useless combinations and in making those which are useful and which are only a small minority. Invention is discernment, choice.*

Koestler highlights the way that creativity is not only involved in artistic originality and scientific discovery – it is also involved in humour. As he points out in *The Act of Creation*, humour or comedy very often involves the bringing

---

* J. S. Bruner *On Knowing: Essays for the Left Hand*

together of two 'mutually exclusive associative contexts'.
Koestler gives the following example:

> Chamfort tells a story of a Marquis at the Court of Louis
> XIV who, on entering his wife's boudoir and finding her in
> the arms of a Bishop, walked calmly to the window and went
> through the motions of blessing the people in the street.
> 'What are you doing?' cried the anguished wife.
> 'Monseigneur is performing my function,' replied the
> Marquis, 'so I am performing his.'

Another example of this is given in *Conceptual
Blockbusting*:

> A woman at a formal dinner was quite discomforted to
> observe that the man across from her was piling his sliced
> carrots carefully upon his head. She watched with horror as
> the pile grew higher and higher and sauce began to drip from
> his hair. She could finally stand it no longer, so she leaned
> toward him and said, 'Pardon me, sir, but why on earth are
> you piling your carrots on your head?'
> 'My God', said he. 'Are they carrots? I thought they were
> sweet potatoes.'

The author of the above book points out that he has usually
found that creative individuals in groups have also been very
humorous, while Maslow is also complimentary about
creative people: '. . . they live far more in the real world of
nature than in the verbalized world of concepts, abstractions,
expectations, beliefs and stereotypes that most people confuse
with the real world . . .'*
Koestler stresses the need for rightist thinking in creative
thinking:

> The creative act, in so far as it depends on unconscious
> resources, presupposes a relaxing of the controls and a
> regression to modes of ideation which are indifferent to the

---

* A. H. Maslow *Toward a Psychology of Being*

rules of verbal logic, unperturbed by contradiction, untouched by the dogmas and taboos of so-called commonsense. At the decisive stage of discovery the codes of disciplined reasoning are suspended – as they are in the dream, the reverie, the manic flight of thought, when the stream of ideation is free to drift by its own emotional gravity, as it were, in an apparently 'lawless' fashion.*

After this initial rightist inspiration, leftist thinking is usually required to implement or follow through the creative insight. It has often been pointed out that in any creative accomplishment, one per cent is inspiration and ninety-nine per cent is application.

How creative are people? One creativity test used is called the Alternate Use Test. The reader might like to try such a test himself. Simply jot down on a sheet of paper all the possible uses you can think of for a *brick* in one minute.

On this test most people will come up with only six or seven uses. When one considers some of man's scientific and artistic breakthroughs, when one considers the complexity of the human brain, such a small number of possible uses for a brick in a minute seems a little disappointing! People who score well on this test tend to come up with more than a few rather bizarre uses for a brick.

When people hear the word 'uses', many impose upon themselves the idea of existing or good uses. This is not what the test requests. The word used was simply 'uses'. If a person relies on leftist thinking the uses he or she will come up with will be existing ones. This typically logical approach will come up with ideas like 'building walls, houses, office blocks' and so on. To come up with more uses (and quite often original and practical uses) try relying upon more rightist thinking. Move away from the ordinary associations you have with bricks and try any and all new associations.

* Arthur Koestler *The Act of Creation*

One fascinating way to try this exercise is with a group. Ask each of the members of the group to jot down one object which he or she thinks bears no relationship whatsoever to a brick. You then ask the group as a whole to try and find some relationship, some use for which the unrelated object can be put in relation to a brick. For example, somebody might come up with the idea of a cigarette and immediately someone in the group will suggest the idea of using a brick as an ashtray! Another person will come up with the idea of a light bulb. The group may suggest having a brick by the side of the bed is a lazy and rich man's way of putting a light out, by simply throwing it at the lightbulb!

To score well in this type of test you simply think of uses *after* you have made the link with any object. By doing this you come up with many more uses and sometimes original and amusing ones. This random-linking idea partly conflicts with J. S. Bruner's opinion on creativity. He argues that 'a welter of permutation' is not the way to come up with 'effective surprise'. Many of the links will give rise to uses which do not offer an effective surprise, but sometimes a new idea will be thrown up. This type of exercise reduces the way that leftist thinking normally comes up with the usual or the ordinary idea – the logical use. Major scientific theory, when first suggested, may seem bizarre or ridiculous. It is only in retrospect that its use may be appreciated.

This type of linking exercise can be built into the problem solving approach (see pp 115). It has already been suggested that at Stage 2 of the process, when you are jotting down all the possible solutions or decisions, it is important to accept even those that seem to be ridiculous or outlandish. Over and above this, you can try introducing a random link. To illustrate this with an example, recently I was running a seminar with a group of managers in industry. The problem we were discussing involved waste. Their particular production system produced a lot of solvent and general waste. The problem was how effectively to dispose of the waste. Having come up with all the possible solutions to the problem, a random link was introduced. In this case the link was 'banana'. Immediately the group pointed out that a banana carries waste – its skin. Therefore they considered how people normally get rid of banana skins! Banana skins may rot; in their case the solvent was too toxic simply to be buried or disposed of so easily. Banana skins could also be burnt. This was an idea that the group had previously not thought of, and was subsequently added to the list of feasibilities. The banana skin idea gave a slightly new perspective to the problem.

Bruner points out that 'creative products have this power of re-ordering experience and thought in their image'. Many problems involve the need of a new perspective, a totally fresh way of looking at the problem. This in part is what is being encouraged in the concept of lateral thinking. Edward de Bono is one of the best-known advocates of lateral thinking, which tries to get away from the predetermined powers of logical or 'vertical' thinking.

Religions and mysticism

Many religions are concerned with the idea of 'enlightenment'. In Hinduism there is Brahman – the ultimate reality. Awareness of Brahman surpasses language and, it is argued, cannot be described in language: 'Incomprehensible is that supreme Soul, unlimited, unborn, not to be reasoned about, unthinkable.' Buddhists seek 'Nirvana'. The Chinese call this reality, 'the Tao'. In Zen, enlightenment is known as 'Satori'. This enlightened conception goes beyond language. Language perception fragments the world into words, things, objects and ideas.

There seem to be two main ways of reducing or rather overcoming fragmented language-orientated perception. One way is through quietening the rational or leftist approach to the world. The major way to do this is through some form of mind quietening or meditation exercise. The other way to surpass language is to become aware of the limitation of language. In Zen, disciples are encouraged to dwell upon 'Koans', intriguing and often contradictory riddles. One of the best known of these riddles is 'What is the sound of one hand clapping?' After much effort to solve the riddle, the student may relinquish and so surpass language.

Meditation exercises take various forms. Many involve some form of relaxed awareness or concentration on a sound, an image or an idea. Perception is often freshened after such exercise. Conventional ways of seeing and thinking can be partly or totally dismantled so as to induce a more real and immediate perception. (This idea seems to be similar to that expressed by the poet Blake in 'The Cleansing of the Doors of Perception'.) Although leftist, analytical, language-orientated, and conceptualising thinking can be associated with Western culture and certain industrialised nations it is misleading and I think wrong to associate the mystical awareness of enlightenment with rightist thinking. However, the development of heightened mystical awareness does in part involve overcoming certain characteristics of leftist thinking.

Ornstein draws a parallel between mystical awareness and new trends in psychology and therapy. In particular he refers to 'gestalt' therapy and psychosynthesis. In gestalt therapy the tendency to be constantly thinking as opposed to experiencing is given the marvellously derogatory term of 'computing'. In gestalt therapy patients are encouraged to be much more *immediately* aware. This therapy also recognises the two types of thinking, leftist and rightist, though in this case left and right refer to the hands and not the brain:

> The right hand is usually the motoric, male, aggressive side that wants to control, to determine what is, to decide what is 'right'. The left side is the female side; it is usually poorly coordinated. *Left* means awkward in many languages:

Gauche in French, *linkisch* in German. When there is a conflict between emotional life and active life, there is neurosis . . . But when both power and sensitivity are working in coordination, there is genius . . . Ultimate awareness can only take place if the computer is gone, if the intuition, the awareness is so bright that one really comes to his senses. The empty mind in Eastern philosophy is worthy of highest praise. So lose your mind and come to your senses.*

Julian Jaynes in his book *The Origin of Consciousness and The Breakdown of the Bicameral Mind* suggests that consciousness as we know it is of comparatively recent origin. Prior to the *Iliad* man was not conscious in the sense that we understand consciousness and his life was controlled by God-like voices which Jaynes associates with the right hemisphere. 'The language of men was involved with only one hemisphere in order to leave the other free for the language of gods.' Furthermore he argues that the differences between the styles of thinking in the hemispheres reflects the differences between man and god. He points out that 'The function of the gods was chiefly the guiding and planning of action in novel situations. The gods size up problems and organise action according to an ongoing pattern or purpose, . . . fitting all the disparate parts together, planting times, harvest times, the sorting out of commodities, all the vast putting together of things in a grand design, and the giving of the directions to the neurological man in his verbal, analytical sanctuary in the left hemisphere. We might thus predict that one residual function of the right hemisphere today would be an organisational one, that of sorting out the experiences of a civilisation and fitting them together into a pattern that could "tell" the individual what to do. Perusal of various speeches of gods in the *Iliad*, the Old Testament, or other ancient literatures is in agreement with this. Different events, past and future, are sorted out,

* J. Fagen and I. L. Shephard (eds) *Gestalt Therapy Now*

categorized, synthesized into a new picture, often with that
ultimate synthesis of a metaphor. And these functions should,
therefore, characterize the right hemisphere.

'The right hemisphere, perhaps like the gods, sees parts as
having a meaning only within a context; it looks at wholes.
While the left, or dominant hemisphere, like the man side of the
bicameral mind, looks at parts themselves.'

Are opposites opposite?

Opposites are caused, some argue, by a leftist way of thinking.
Because we think in terms of opposites we may also think in
terms of conflicts. A list of opposites could include life versus
death, reason versus passion, logic versus intuition, sacred
versus profane, conscious versus unconscious, male versus
female, left versus right, time versus space, verbal versus
spatial or intellect versus mind. The list can go on almost
indefinitely:

> ... it is elementary that concepts derive their meanings in
> relation to their opposites, that X means something in
> relation to non-X. We have been made familiar with this idea
> from Heraclitus to Hegel. So it is not surprising that we find
> in the languages of the peoples we study words which can be
> set forth in pairs of complementary opposites, eg dark and
> light, hot and cold, good and bad, and so on . . .*

Alan Watts, an excellent interpreter of Eastern mysticism
for the Western mind, quite simply points out that 'there is no
on without off, no up without down'.**

In the terms of one psychologist, 'the occurrence of so many
terminological dichotomies is not obviously related to the
bilateral symmetry of the brain but can be ascribed to a nearly

---

* R. Needham (ed) *Right and Left*
** A. Watts *The Book on the Taboo Against Knowing Who You Are*

universal predilection for the logical simplicity of a binary system'.* From an anthropological point of view the same tendency is described as 'a dualistic categorization of phenomena of which this opposition is paradigmatic, are so common as to seem natural proclivites of the human mind'.** One researcher has suggested that the tendency for the human mind to work in terms of opposites may not simply be explained in terms of the 'logical simplicity of a binary system' but rather that 'this predilection is itself one expression of the duality of the minds'.†

If a concept derives its meaning from its opposite, is it not possible to see the relation between opposites as complementary as opposed to conflicting? An interesting example is that of male and female. If one thinks of mankind not as a mass of individuals but as a continuing species, the male and female are not only complementary, they are essential for the continuation of the species. On the physical complementariness of the sexes Alan Watts graphically points out that 'Obviously, the male has the convex penis and the female the concave vagina; and though people have regarded the former as a possession and the latter as a deprivation, any fool should be able to recognise that one cannot have the outstanding without the instanding, and that a rampant *membrum virile* is no good without somewhere to put it, and vice versa.'††

Another very general, possible conflicting opposite is that of the whole versus the part. Western science and analysis tends particularly towards describing and analysing the part. Watts points out that

---

* R. H. Ornstein (ed) *The Nature of Human Consciousness*
** R. Needham (ed) *Right and Left* p7
† R. H. Ornstein (ed) *The Nature of Human Consciousness*
†† A. Watts *The Tao: The Watercourse Way*

... It is not enough ... to describe, define, and try to understand things or events by analysis alone ... Today, scientists are more and more aware that what things are, and what they are doing, depends on where and when they are doing it. If, then, the definition of a thing or event must include definition of its environment, we realize that any given thing *goes with* a given environment so intimately and inseparably that it is more and more difficult to draw a clear boundary between the thing and its surroundings.*

To understand the whole by studying its parts is, to use the often given analogy, like trying to understand an artist's masterpiece by scrutinising it in a dark room with a pen torch. The artist, in painting a picture, while concentrating on detail, is aware of the whole. Having finished a detail in the painting, the artist stands back and takes it in in its entirety.

Language gives rise to a fragmented way of thinking and perceiving. It may reduce one's ability to see the interrelatedness of a given situation. This point is well illustrated in the following Sufi story:

'What is fate?' Nasrudin was asked by a scholar.
'An endless succession of intertwined events, each influencing the others.'
'That is hardly a satisfactory answer. I believe in cause and effect!'
'Very well,' said the Mulla, 'look at that.' He pointed to a procession passing in the street.
'That man is being taken to be hanged. Is that because someone gave him a silver piece and enabled him to buy the knife with which he committed the murder; or because someone saw him do it; or because nobody stopped him?'**

Simply to consider the world in terms of language and, in this case, in terms of cause and effect, can give a limited picture.

* A. Watts *The Book on the Taboo Against Knowing Who You Are*
** Idris Shah *The Exploits of the Incomparable Mulla Nasrudin*

There is also possible conflict between the linear concept of time and the non-linear concept of the ever present *now*. Excessive leftist thinking can encourage constant 'computing'. The person may never be thinking about what he is doing at the moment he is doing it. He may simply be thinking about something he has done or a particular idea of what he has to do later. This type of thinking may be very aware of a past and be very involved in planning the future, but there may be little awareness of the present moment. Immediate sensual enjoyment may therefore be reduced.

The anthropologist, Dorothy Lee, reports that the natives of the Trobriand Islands live very much in the present, and that this is reflected in their language. With a greater awareness of now, there is less emphasis, unlike in our leftist thinking, on the 'flow' of time. Things have a status in their own right and are not simply parts of a chain of cause and effect or towards a particular purpose. For example, a pregnancy in most peoples minds means a forthcoming birth. Congratulations will follow the birth. 'Among the Trobrianders pregnancy has a meaning in itself, as a state of being.'*

Fig. 18

* R. H. Ornstein (ed) *The Nature of Human Consciousness*

The idea of yin and yang is often cited as an illustration of the complementary nature of opposites (Fig. 18). 'The principal characteristic of the *Tao* is the cyclic nature of its ceaseless motion and chance . . . The idea of cyclic patterns in the motion of the Tao was given a definite structure by the introduction of the polar opposites yin and yang.'* The two small spots represent the idea that if one extreme is reached the seed of the opposite is already present. Yang represents the strong, the creative male while yin represents the dark, the feminine and the receptive. Yin and yang are important in the Chinese concept of diet, medicine and in *I Ching – The Book of Changes*:

The key to the relationship between *yang* and *yin* is called *hsiang sheng*, mutual arising or inseparability. As Lao-tzu puts it,
'When everyone knows beauty as beautiful, there is already ugliness;
When everyone knows good as goodness, there is already evil.
"To be" and "not to be" arise mutually; Difficult and easy are mutually realized; Long and short are mutually contrasted; High and low are mutually posited; . . . Before and after are in mutual sequence.'**

Opposites are therefore seen as complementary.

The idea of complementarity has come to the fore in physics. This can be simply illustrated in asking the question 'what is colour?' This question caused a dispute between Goethe and Newton. Newton's explanation was scientific while Goethe's was more sensuous. Both descriptions are needed to give a full answer.

For hundreds of years physics developed or rather imposed

---

* F. Capra *The Tao of Physics*
** A. Watts *The Tao: The Watercourse Way*

various laws on the natural world by analysing parts of that world. Physicists today however, recognise the interconnected, interrelated and interdependent nature of any one phenomenon.

Another example of complementarity in physics is the dual interpretation of light as being either waves or particles. Both descriptions are correct. The descriptions are different ways of describing the same reality.

The individual and society

In a highly industrialised society an individual can become a victim of society's bureaucracy and technology. Since the 1960s there have been various trends which collectively have been referred to as the 'counter culture'.* In part this counter culture shows an increased interest in the intuitive, the magical, the sensuous. There has been a rightist reaction to excessive leftism. Various trends seem to have been part of this general rightist reaction, from the 'flower-power' era of the 1960s through to calls for humanising of industrial processes. In many ways an excessively leftist approach, some argue, gives rise to a world hell-bent on annihilating itself. A 'full grasp', interrelated perception (rightist thinking) lies at the centre of increasing ecological awareness.

Scientists recognise that a biological system cannot be treated in isolation. Medicine increasingly recognises that a specific illness needs to be considered in the light of the whole body. We are beginning to reassemble the isolated pieces of our jigsaw and by using our more rightist thinking grasp the whole interrelated nature of man and his environment. Man and his environment, man and his society are seen as being totally interdependent. The research on the left and right hemispheres quickly caught the public's imagination. One reason for this is that the apparent functions of the hemispheres may help to

* T. Roszak *The Makings of a Counter-Culture*

explain the imbalance that many people saw and see in modern society, a society which is bureaucratic, over-industrialised, and over-structured.

A society which is only leftist in its thinking, although highly developed in some ways, needs to develop its more sensuous 'whole grasp' intuitive perception. Societies that have been too rightist in their thinking, on the other hand, have tended to disintegrate through lack of order and system.

Individual perception is heightened through the using and blending of leftist and rightist thinking. A newly born child understands his world in an immediate 'whole grasp' way. As he grows up and develops powers of language and logic he fragments his perceptions. He may start computing and fail to live in the present. Today he is planning tomorrow; tomorrow, he will be planning the day after. The present moment never arrives. The first state is that of innocence, the second of experience. A few people regain innocence. Slowly a person can re-establish the innocent all-grasping perception. The child's innocence can be compared to a first glance at a rich and massive canvas. Experience comes by looking closely at the technique, the detail and the contrast of a painting. This is the stage at which many people stay. The observer then stands back, and does not simply regain his original whole grasp of the painting. He finds that his perception is all the richer for his having been aware of the detail, of the parts.

The distinctions I have made between the left and right hemispheres and between rightist and leftist thought, are in themselves typical of leftist thinking. It may be convenient to pull things to pieces in order to examine, analyse and categorise, but it is also important to see how the whole works, and to see that it only consists of parts because we choose to pull it to pieces.

A bringing together and developing of leftist and rightist complementary thinking and perception is well illustrated by the ancient symbol of joined hands in prayer.

Bibliography

Adams, J. L. *Conceptual Blockbusting*, W. H. Freeman, 1974

Bailey, R. H. *The Role of the Brain*, Time Life Books, 1970

Barsley, M. *The Left-Handed Book*, Pan, 1966

Blakemore, C. *The Mechanics of the Mind*, Cambridge University Press, 1977

Brown, M. E. *Memory Matters*, David & Charles, 1977

Bruner, J. S. *On Knowing: Essays for the Left Hand*, Belknap Press, 1962

Buzan, T. *Use your Head*, BBC Publications, 1974

Capra, F. *The Tao of Physics*, Fontana Collins, 1976

Carroll, L, ed Gardner, M. *The Annotated Alice*, Penguin Books, revised 1972

Corballis, M. C. and Beale, I. L. *The Psychology of Left and Right*, Lawrence Erlbaum Associates, 1976

Corner, A. C. *Cerebral Lateralisation of Verbal and Spatial Functions: Relations with Reading Ability and Handedness in Young People* unpublished dissertation, 1977

de Bono, E. *The Mechanism of Mind*, Penguin Books, reprinted 1977

Dimond, S. J. *The Double Brain*, Churchill Livingstone, 1972

Dimond, S. J. and Beaumont, G. J. *Hemisphere Function in the Human Brain*, Elek Science, 1974

Douglas, Mary *Natural Symbols: Explorations in Cosmology*, Barrie & Jenkins, 1970

Fagen, J. and Shephard, I. L. (eds) *Gestalt Therapy Now*, Harper & Row, 1971

Gardner, M. *The Ambidextrous Universe*, Science and Discovery Books, 1964

Gregory, R. L. *Eye and Brain*, World University Library, 1972 edition

Hayakawa, S. I. *Language in Thought and Action*, George Allen & Unwin, second impression, 1977

Hoffmann, B. and Dukas, H. *Albert Einstein*, Paradin, reprinted 1977

Huxley, A. *The Doors of Perception*, Panther, 1977

Kinsbourne, M. and Smith, W. L. (eds) *Hemispheric Disconnection and Cerebral Function*, Charles C. Thomas, 1974

Koestler, A. *The Act of Creation*, Picador, 1975

Koestler, A. *The Ghost in the Machine*, Picador, 1975

Lausch, E. *Manipulation*, Fontana/Collins, 1975

Luria, A. R. *The Working Brain*, Allen Lane, The Penguin Press, reprinted 1976

Maslow, A. H. *Toward a Psychology of Being*, Van Nostrand, second edition, 1968

McKim, R. H. *Experiences in Visual Thinking*, Monteray: Brooks/Cole, 1972

Needham, R. (ed) *Right and Left: Essays on Dual Symbolic Classifications*, University of Chicago Press, 1973

O'Neill, J. J. *Prodigal Genius: The Life of Nikola Tesla*, Spearman 1968

Ornstein, R. H. (ed) *The Nature of Human Consciousness*, W. H. Freeman, 1973

Ornstein, R. H. *The Psychology of Consciousness*, W. H. Freeman, 1972

Ounsted and Taylor (eds) *Gender Differences: Their Ontogeny and Significance*, Churchill Livingstone, 1972

Roszak, T. *Sources*, Harper Colophon Books, 1972

Roszak, T. *The Making of a Counter-Culture*, Faber & Faber, reprinted 1972

Russell, P. *The TM Technique*, Routledge & Kegan Paul, 1976

Snow, C. P. *The Two Cultures: And A Second Look*, Cambridge University Press, 1969

Wall, W. D. *Constructive Education for Adolescents*, Unesco, Harrap, 1977

Watson, J. D. *The Double Helix*, Penguin Books, reprinted 1971

Watts, A. *Nature, Man and Woman*, Abacus, 1976

Watts, A. *The Book on the Taboo Against Knowing Who You Are*, Abacus, 1973

Watts, A. *The Tao: The Watercourse Way*, Cape, 1975

Widroe, H. J. *Human Behaviour and Brain Function*, Charles C. Thomas, 1975

Courses

Courses run along the lines of this book and of *Memory Matters* (David & Charles, 1977) are run by the author throughout Europe. Details may be obtained by writing to the author at 15 Osten Mews, London SW7 4HW.

Index

Adams, James, 114
African tribes, right and left in, 40-1
Alternate Use Test, 120
ambidexterity, 28, 38
Ambidextrous Universe, The (Gardner), 14, 20
anablebs, asymmetry of, 14
animals, paw preference, 30-1
artist versus scientist, 97-8
asymmetrical creatures, 14
asymmetry, 14-16

back-front reflection, 20
Bacon, Sir Francis, 32
Barsley, Michael, 38, 40
bath water, preference for left or right, 16
Benjamin, left-handed men in army of, 30
Berger, Hans, 64
Blakemore, Colin, 111
brain:
  left, 65-6; right, 66-70;
  right and left hemispheres, 59-64;
  structure of, 49-52;
  at work, 71-5
brain damage:
  and left-handedness, 37-8, 39;
  research and, 63
brain waves, 64

brainedness, and handedness, 80-2
brains, two, purpose of specialization of, 86-9
Bruner, J. S., 98, 118, 121, 122
Butler, Stuart, 85

Carroll, Lewis, and mirror writing, 26-7
Chelhod, J., 32
Chien-Shiung Wu, Madame, 16
coriolis effect, 16
creativity, 118-22
criminal, left-handedness considered sign of, 17, 37

Darwin, Charles, 110
Deikman, Arthur, 117
Domhoff, William, 44
dominant eye, 14

education, 102-5
Edwards, Betty, 104
Einstein, Albert, 99
electric shocks, unilateral, 61-3
'emotional negativism', as cause of left-handedness, 36-7
emotional associations, 17-18
environment, effect on handedness, 31-3
eye, dominant, 14

'flopping' experiment, 27

football machine mystery, 83-6
Freud, Sigmund, 19, 72

Gardner, Martin, 14, 17, 20, 27, 37, 38
George VI, 30
Ghost in the Machine, The (Koestler), 98
glucose, as guide to left or right, 14
Graves, Robert, 39
Greek Myths (Graves), 39

handedness:
and brainedness, 80-2;
danger of forcing switch of, 30;
determination of, 28-30;
environment or heredity, 31-55;
genetic influence, 33-5
hearing tests, 63
heart, as guide to left or right, 14
Helmholtz, Hermann von, 19
heredity, effect on handedness, 33-5
hermit crab, asymmetry of, 14
Herron, Jeannine, 76
Hertz, Robert, 17-18, 36, 43, 45
Holbein, Hans, 39
honeysuckle, left-handed climbing of, 14
Huxley, Aldous, 101
hygiene, handedness in, 41, 43

imagery, 114

Jackson, Hughlings, 59
Jaynes, Julian, 73, 124

Kerr family, and reputation for left-handedness, 34-5
Kinsbourne, Marcel, 79
Kipling, Rudyard, 91
Koestler, Arthur, 98, 118-20
Kruyt, Alb, 42

language:
tests for, 78-80;
and thought, 98-102
learning, 105-10
Lee, Dorothy, 128
left and right:
definitions of, 16-19;
difficulties of establishing, 18-19;
emotive associations, 17-18;
political connotations, 18;
symbolism of, 95-7
left hand:
taboos against, 41, 43-4;
as unfavoured hand, 17, · 35-8, 40-4
left-handedness:
advantages and disadvantages, 38-9;
expressions for, 40;
increase in, 29-30;
misconceptions over, 17, 36-8;
reasons for, 37-8
left-handers, and processing of language, 75-7
Leonardo da Vinci, 39; as mirror writer, 27
Levy, Jerry, 30, 89
liver, as basis for handedness, 32
Lombroso, Cesare, 36

male, superiority over female in spatial tasks, 82-3
Maslow, A. H., 102

meditation, 122-3
Michelangelo, 39
mirror problem, 19-27
mirror writing, 27-8
mysticism, 122-4
mythology, 39-44

nature, intrinsic handedness of, 14-16
'Nuer Spear Symbolism' (Pritchard), 41

Ornstein, Robert, 86, 95, 103, 123-4

Pavlov, Ivan, 74
paw preference, 30-1
Plato, 33
Poincaré, Henri, 100
poles, as 'opposite sides of a spin', 16
political connotations, 18
primitive man:
    and opposites, 43;
    right-handedness in, 31
Prior, Andrew J., 84, 86
Pritchard, Evans, 41
problem solving, 114-18
Psychology of Consciousness, The (Ornstein), 95

Ravel, Maurice, 63
reading from left to right, 27
reflection, in mirror, 19-27

religions, 122-4
reversal in mirror, 19-27
'right':
    definitions of, 16-19;
    emotive associations, 17-18
right hand, as favoured hand, 17-18, 30-3, 35-8, 40
Russell, Bertrand, 117

scenic photographs, 'flopping' of, 27
semantic differential test, 42-3
Snow, C. P., 97, 102
specialization, 110-11
Sperry, Roger, 53, 57
split-brain patients, 52-9
sport, left-handedness in, 38-9
sun, association with right side, 31-2, 39
superstitions, 39-44
'sword and shield' theory, 32

Tesla, Nikola, 100
thought, and language, 98-102
'tonic neck reflex', 34
tornadoes, influenced by traffic flow, 16
Two Cultures, The (Snow), 97

visual tests, 64

Watts, Alec, 125-7
Wieschoff, Heinz, 41